Thirty-Eight Church Revitalization Models for the Twenty-First Century!

By
Tom Cheyney

CreateSpace
A division of Amazon.com

First published by Renovate Publishing Group in
10/4/2014.

ISBN: 0990781607

ISBN: 978-0-9907816-0-8

Printed in the United States of America

Dedication

To Cheryl, my beloved!

My best friend, life companion, and one who challenges me every day to be the best I can for my Lord. You mean the world to me. There are so many things I truly admire about you as a person, as my best friend and as my wife. Your smile lights up my soul. As a church revitalizer's wife, you have been courageous to go even when the path seemed unclear and yet the hand of God was certain. You have given much and sacrificed more so others might see Jesus.

To all of those Church Revitalizers serving in local churches asking God to do great things once more and revive their church once more. The course is not easy, but the need is great and our Master longs to see the church restored for future generations.

"For God has not given us a spirit of fearfulness, but one of power, love, and sound judgment"
2 Timothy 1:7 HCSB

To God be the glory forever and ever.

What Others Are Saying About *Thirty-Eight Church Revitalization Models For the Twenty-first Century*!

Tom Cheyney knows churches. As a church leader himself and as an advisor to countless pastors, Tom has developed insights about church life and health which are valuable resources for all of us. In particular, Tom has a heart for church revitalization, which is one of the most pressing issues of our day. I am thankful for the investment Tom has made in helping pastors and other leaders breathe new life into dying and declining congregations.

Michael Duduit, Executive Editor of Preaching Magazine and founding Dean of the Clamp Divinity School at Anderson University in Anderson, SC)

When it comes to church revitalization there is not a "one size fits all" approach that will work. Church revitalization is a process. Dr. Cheyney, in this book, does an outstanding job presenting the different revitalization models that a church can apply to its unique situation. I highly recommend this book to anyone who has a desire to see the church experience renewed vision and passion.

Larry Wynn, Vice President, Church Revitalization, Georgia Baptist Convention

Tom Cheyney brings to light his expertise in revitalization in this new work. No two churches are alike, and as such, no two revitalizations are truly alike. Evaluating an appropriate model for your context is needed; and with these "Thirty-Eight Church Revitalization Models for the Twenty-First Century" pastors can discover where their respective church is and determine the best model for moving forward. You will want to read what Tom has provided and address turnaround in a biblical perspective in your church.

Kenneth Priest, Director Convention Strategies Southern Baptists of Texas Convention

When you think of church revitalization, what comes to mind? Most people in ministry can identify two or three models of church revitalization. However, there are many more options out there for plateaued and declining churches. Dr. Tom Cheyney, who is quickly becoming known as the father of the church revitalization movement, has identified Thirty-Eight Church Revitalization Models for the Twenty-First Century in his new book of the same title. Readers will discover that much more is being done in the area of church revitalization than previously realized. Each of these models are carefully explained so that church leaders can see what may work best in their situation. Inspiring and hopeful, this is a must read for anyone who is concerned about the state of churches in North America.

Mark Weible, Director of Church Planting Greater Orlando Baptist Association

My friend Tom Cheyney has spent the last 35 years serving with the church planting and church revitalization movement. Although he speaks nationally about church growth, Tom is still in the middle of coaching and leading pastors in his own association of Orlando. For me personally, I learn volumes from those that are in the trenches here and now. This recent research on church models is exactly what leaders need to customize and apply these principles to their own people and community. In church life, many pastors are at the crossroads that can determine success or failure. In this new book, Tom provides some great resources for a pastor's journey to lead and grow!

Neil Franks, Lead Pastor FBC Branson - (Developer of the 2-Minute Pastor Daily Video Devotional App)

Tom Cheney is like few in this world on Church Revitalization. He thinks about and integrates into his life and ministry the principles of this book quicker than you and I click the refresh image and update our technology toy. The man KNOWS and APPLIES what he writes...like what you have before you. As you read and mark this work up, PRAY, THINK, REFLECT, INTEGRATE AND APPLY...and of course, REFRESH in a healthy way.

Greg Kappas, President, Grace Global Network & Vice President, The Timothy Initiative Author Five Stages for Multiplying Healthy Churches

When facing the daunting task of turning your church around, starting from scratch is difficult. Dr. Tom Cheyney has brought together some of the best models for the successful "Revitalization" of your church. This is the resource to have if you are serious about effectively "turning your situation around." Tom is a real Pastor's Pastor and has a heart for your crucial role in finding a new beginning for your church. Whether you are a Senior Pastor, or a church leadership team, this is a must read!

Rob Myers, Pastor of Miami Baptist Church of Miami Florida and radio personality with his International Program: The Xristos Factor, President and founder of Baptist World Charities: A Global Missions Community

Thirty-Eight Church Revitalization Models for the 21st Century provides pastors and church leaders with the framework necessary to build a revitalization strategy for the church. Today, when nearly 80% of churches are plateaued or declining, Tom Cheyney's resource highlights proven models for revitalization. Tom's heart for revitalization along with years of teaching revitalization uniquely qualify him to share these models. No other book so clearly provides an overview of the models that are being used to restore the church to sustainability and vitality. I heartily recommend this book to any pastor or leader who is seeking to restore vitality and vision to the church.

Rodney Harrison, Co-Author of Spinoff Churches

When it comes to church revitalization, Tom should be considered a guru. The perspective he brings is incredibly helpful and challenging for anyone who is or wants to be involved in a church revitalization project. He does not just offer general concepts that are great in theory. Tom's passion for existing churches causes him to go beyond the general ideas and present solid, practical revitalization steps anyone can take.

Jason Cooper, Pastor & Church Revitalizer of Church @ Oak Level

Tom Cheyney is the seminal leader in the Church Revitalization Movement in America today. His vast experience as a church planter and revitalizer, coupled with his ability to communicate within both academia and to the church, uniquely qualifies him to write the official playbook of revitalization strategies. In *Thirty-Eight Church Revitalization Models for the 21st Century*, Cheyney has comprehensively identified and described the contemporary strategies for addressing church revitalization. Church leaders who are looking for guidance as they lead their churches into a revitalization process will find this work to be an essential and invaluable tool to guide them in the strategy that best fits their settings.

Terry Rials, Church Revitalizer & Pastor of Crestview Baptist Church

Thirty-Eight Church Revitalization Models for the Twenty-First Century is an important resource for any leader looking to bring about renewal and revitalization in the local Church. There is no debating the fact that the present-day church is in desperate need of renewal and revitalization. Through Cheyney's expertise and experience, you will develop an appreciation for the many ways that God can bring about health and vitality in the church. The stakes are high and the challenge is big, but with the pearls of wisdom you find in this book, you will gain confidence and understanding as a leader in how you can see revitalization in your church for the glory of God.

Dr. Michael Atherton Senior Pastor Cornerstone Church & author of The Revitalized Church

I have known Dr. Tom Cheyney for 25 years. Dr. Cheyney is the best researcher, writer and presenter I know. I first heard Dr. Cheyney speak when he was a pastor on evangelism in California at a missions national meeting 25 years ago. He stays on top of the needs of our churches in real time and always has the answers to the problems plaguing the Church in present day. His book "Spin-off Churches" is the best I have read for a Primary Partnering Church to use as a planting manual. You will not be disappointed with *Thirty-Eight Church Revitalization Models for the Twenty-First Century!*

Jim Brunk, Smaller Attendances Church Outreach Ministries Specialist for the Baptist General Convention of Oklahoma

Tom's passion for existing churches causes him to go beyond the general ideas and present solid, practical revitalization steps anyone can take. Christendom has been inundated with a plethora of revitalization processes and programs. Some are good and some are less than stellar. Dr. Cheyney has produced this work to strategically weigh 38 models of revitalization, so you may determine the healthiest process for your own toolbox. Tom has been on the cutting edge of church revitalization for years, and this book is proof of his expertise and insight concerning the conditions to become a healthy, growing, glorifying church.

Tracy W. Jaggers, Church Development Associate for the Tryon Evergreen Baptist Association in Conroe, Texas

Don't bother searching the Internet to borrow an idea from a church. Tom provides 38 proven and practical models that will help your church. I have three years of experience teaching, leading and podcasting with Tom. These models are extremely practical and intensely researched. No matter where you serve this is a valuable resource to help your church."

Ron Smith, Author of Churches Gone Wild

Acknowledgements

Almost fifteen years ago I wrote a book for the church planting community titled *Twenty-One Church Planting Models for the Twenty-First Century*. Recently, an individual who had that work asked why I had not created a similar book to challenge the church revitalization community. It was a question that challenged me since I deal with the various models almost daily. That began my journey towards creating this tool for churches of all sizes in need of church revitalization and renewal. Each year while working with both churches locally where I live in central Florida and those who I am blessed to have in attendance at the *RENOVATE National Church Revitalization Conference* which I founded, the topic of revitalization models often surface. While there are certainly models that we have shared with our participants, let's be quick to say that there is no magic pill for church revitalization and renewal, and what works in one setting may not work in another. I would like to thank Tracy Jaggers for his contribution in getting me started in the development this book. Additionally, Rodney Harrison, Terry Rials and Mark Weible have been tremendous friends who would allow me to bounce ideas and experiences off of them and they always gave the time for analysis, support, and encouragement.

Forward

The Seven Pillars of
Church Revitalization and Renewal

Our Lord loves the local New Testament Church

and it is His desire to see it grow! The need for Church

Revitalization has never been greater in North

America! An estimated 340,000 Protestant churches in

America have an average attendance of less than one

hundred.[1] Research data tells us that in the United

States more than 80% of the churches have plateaued or

are declining.[2] Each and every week we are currently

seeing somewhere between fifty and seventy-five local

churches closing their doors and not opening them

again. Everything that must be done in the area of

church revitalization cannot be accomplished in a few

hours on the Lord's Day!

---

[1]   Hartford   Institute   for   Religious   Research

The most recent research data released in

January of 2012 by the *Leavell Center for Evangelism and*

Church Health, has indicated that within my own

Southern Baptist Convention we are at a critical

juncture regarding church plateau and decline. The

most recent series of studies have been conducted by

Bill Day, Associate Director of the *Leavell Center for*

Evangelism and Church Health, who serves the New

Orleans Baptist Theological Seminary as the Gurney

Professor of Evangelism and Church Health. Day

conducted sequential studies on church health and

growth in 2003, 2007, and 2010, and in January of 2012

he reported that currently there are less than seven

percent (6.8) of our SBC churches that are healthy

growing churches. That means only 3,087 of our 45,727

(hirr.hartsem.edu/research)

[2] Research Source: Stats listed online at: http://www.newchurchinitiatives.org/morechurches/index.htm (accessed 2/23/2006).

SBC churches are healthy. Even the number of SBC churches is in decline and we need to address the needs for church revitalization immediately.

Thinking About the Seven Pillars of Church Revitalization

Working in the area of Church Revitalization will lead you eventually to consider the Seven Pillars of Church Revitalization. A Church Revitalizer will not be working in all of these areas at the same time, but you will eventually find yourself working in most of them at one time or another. Take a moment to reflect upon the Seven Pillars graph as we discuss these areas of renewal and revitalization.

Revitalization and Realignment

Perhaps the easiest pillar to address is revitalization and realignment. Some observers of church revitalization and renewal argue that the era of small churches is over and that the future belongs to the arising mega churches across North America. Granted, mega is an amazing phenomenon of the past thirty years which seems to have arisen with the concept of the massive campus church. But to ignore the 340,000 plus churches in North America that average less than 100 weekly in church attendance would be ill advised! Those who serve and those who attend these churches are an enormously significant network of Christian influence. Even the mega church finds itself struggling to avoid plateau and decline.

A church in need of Revitalization is described as one where there is the plateauing or declining after a phase of recent or initial expansion followed by: the beginning of a high turn-over of lay leaders, a shorter duration of stay of fully assimilated people within the work, a drop-in church morale and momentum, a brief period of coasting followed by another drop. This cycle of decline is repeated again and again, resulting in a new low! This new normal is the first sign of a church in need.

Refocusing

Refocusing is the second pillar and it helps churches that are growing but that still need to set new challenges and look for new opportunities to expand their gospel witness into their target area. Questions such as: "What is your biblical purpose?", and "Why do we exist as a congregation?" must be addressed. Looking at how God showed up in the past is a good way to get the church unstuck by addressing where it has been, how God has worked, and anticipating what does He holds for its future. Addressing the church's focus, vision, and leading them to discover God's new direction is just the beginning of helping a congregation to begin refocusing towards the Lord's new calling plan for the church! Many a pastor today has never been taught how to grow a church and they feel quite stuck and in need of someone to come along side of them and challenge them to refocus both themselves and the church.

Re-visioning

Re-visioning is a little bit harder certainly, but not as hard as the descending order of decline that will eventually lead to the *Restarting* pillar of revitalization.

Have you ever seen a church that once was alive and vital begin to lose its focus and drive for the cause of Christ? That is a church that needs to work on its Re-visioning strategy! A *Re-visioning* strategy works to help churches dream new dreams and accomplish new goals that lead towards re-growing a healthy church! This strategy is designed for a weekend retreat tailored to fit and foster a sense of ownership and teamwork related to discovering a shared vision for the church. Understanding the critical milestones necessary for a new vision will help foster healthy church practices that might have been lost. Something as simple as achieving a great goal of some sort can begin to launch a church back into a *Re-visioning* strategy. Something as simple and dangerous as the Lord's children taking an ill-advised rest that resulted in a slowing or stalling of the momentum into a maintenance mentality can cause a church to become stuck.

Renewing

Church Renewal is the forth pillar of the seven pillars of Church Revitalization process. Often the church simply needs to get back to that which was working and get back on track. When that is needed, a careful renewal strategy needs to be planned and carried out. Renewing a congregation becomes much harder than the refocusing, re-visioning and revitalization process. Not everyone who works in church renewal is wired the exact same way and it is important to understand each congregation's individual needs and not try to make one size fit all. There is no magic pill in church revitalization. Far too much writing on church growth of the 1980's was designed in a one size fits all "bigger is better" model and while it may not have been the only cause for declining numbers in our churches, it certainly contributed! It is vital that you prepare the laity for the work of church renewal as well as yourself. Communicate early and often with the church how the renewal process will take place and how it will be implemented. Prepare yourself spiritually and then prepare your leaders spiritually. Then begin preparing your church spiritually for renewal! A *Church Renewal Weekend* is a great way to start. Church renewal is not about finding the magic medication or treatment to get growing. It is more about discovering God's vision for the church and practicing it for the long haul. The utilization of a Church Renewal weekend works well to draw God's people back towards health and vitality.

Reinvention

This fifth pillar of Church Revitalization deals with tools and techniques needed in order to assist the church when it is necessary to reinvent itself to a changing community. When a church experiences a shift in the community makeup, often there will be to various degrees, the need to redevelop a new experience for those who make up the new church context! New experiences must replace old experiences. New practices likewise will replace old practices. A church that is experiencing the need for reinvention must take seriously the need and make the commitment for reinventing itself, revaluing itself, reforming itself, and reinvigorating itself to fit the new context.

Restoration

This sixth area of Church Revitalization deals with things a church and a minister must go through when circumstances necessitate that a restoration process is called for! Things such as:

Gaining a new and fresh understanding of the new future for the church is vital if success is in the church's future.

Inspiring new prospects with a vision that is both compelling and motivational. Prospects seek to be inspired and not dragged down in the world in which we live.

Meet new needs in order to give your church a restored place among the community in which you seek to further minister.

Become prospect driven during these days of transition. Look for new and unreached· opportunities to minister.

Remember if you try to do everything, you will end up doing nothing. Therefore, pick your greatest opportunities first and let the rest follow along later.

Craft something that comes out of a community in flux and look for ways to reconnect to the community where you once were firmly entrenched. Keep in mind you have been given a second chance, so don't blow it! Prayerfully seek the new things because it might be something you will be doing for a long long time.

Restarting

The final Pillar of Church Revitalization is the hardest, and often only happens once the church's patriarchs and matriarchs have tried everything else they could think of to grow the church with no success! The challenge here is that most churches wait too long to enter into this area of revitalization and by the time they are willing to utilize this strategy, they have sucked out all of the life within the church and it is no longer a viable candidate for this effort. When a sick church no longer has the courage to work through the various issues that led to its poor health, it is usually identified as being on life support and in need of a restart. This type of church has been flat-lined and just holding on by means of its legacy and the faithful few who attend. The Restarting Strategy (also known as a Repotting strategy) is for an unhealthy church to once again begin growing and to engage in a renewed vision that is demonstrated through sufficient evidences of hope. The restart-based church revitalization model is being used all across North America. Any group planting churches or working in the area of Church Revitalization should have a restart strategy if it is going to be a wise steward. One critical point from the start is that a complete change of leadership and direction is a must for this revitalization model to be successful. Lyle Schaller reminds us that 85,000 evangelical churches are running fewer than 50 on Sunday. Being aware of their "critical" condition, however, is not enough. They must become convinced they need "major" surgical treatment. One church I have worked with still believes that they have more to offer though their decline has been meteoritic, and yet they refuse to allow a restart to take place.

Changing the mindset of the residual membership can often be very difficult. Senior adults occupy most of these churches that are candidates for a restart, and for which change is often hard to come by. Until the church is ready to make drastic changes, it is useless to become involved. There are thousands of churches like this all over America: Some are Baptists, others are Methodists, even in the Assemblies you can find them, Presbyterians, the Lutherans have them, Congregational, Christian, and many others, waiting for a mission-minded congregation to get involved in offering "new life."

One startling phenomena in some churches today is that as the laity begin to depart this life, they often see nothing wrong with taking the church to the grave as well. That was never part of God's plan for the very thing for which He gave up His life.

Introduction

There is an ample assortment of terms that a Church Revitalizer and local church working in renewal can use. The three main terms that are often used interchangeably are:

Church Revitalization Models

Church Revitalization Designs

Church Revitalization Strategies

Perhaps the best term for church revitalization and renewal is a mixture of at least two. Think about the term Church Revitalization Models/Designs. How about Church Revitalization Strategy Designs? Which one works for you? The new century in which we minister requires a passion and courage of apostolic style and individuals who are courageous enough to reach out to a lost and dying world. While church planting remains the single most effective means for evangelism, there needs to be a re-awakening and redirection towards church revitalization and renewal, if we desire to see the mainline church to continue to flourish. Christians and the greater evangelical community are responsible for the declining church. What we can do and ought to do, in and through the declining church, we must do. Otherwise we have the demise of the western church on our heads. If the declining church needs our evangelical community to offer assistance, then the evangelical community needs the declining church more. In the past, the trained minister was a by-product of the various denominations. Yet today the skill set necessary for a church revitalizer to be successful are far from understood in most denominational headquarters.

What Does Church Revitalization Mean?

Church Revitalization is a movement within protestant evangelicalism, which emphasizes the missional work of turning a plateaued, declining, or rapidly declining church around and moving it back towards growth and health. Churches today are losing the corporate memory from the past of how to actually turnaround a church.

Often that means that what we did to revitalize churches in the twentieth century might not work in the twenty-first century. Much of the practices and methodologies of the bigger is better church growth movement of the early 1980's up to the mid 1990's has not brought about significant, longstanding health if any at all. As leaders of church revitalization and renewal, our prayer is that God will raise up an army of missional individuals like the apostle Paul who will preach Christ and revitalize healthy evangelical churches across North America. Far too many church renewal efforts fail because the church revitalizer follows a model that may have worked elsewhere instead of seeking God's face about a new unique and perhaps unprecedented model required for that particular challenge and situation.

While some church revitalizers see church revitalization models as mere fable, others see the validity of having examples and samples to study in the effort to get a glimpse of what God might be saying about how to bring church renewal to their present work! Regardless of the debate regarding myths for models or strategies for the revitalization churches, there appears to be at least six areas and thirty-eight strategies that a church seeking renewal could consider as they begin to turn around the ministry of the local church. For further understanding of the field of church revitalization and renewal, consider attending the *RENOVATE National Church Revitalization Conference*, which meets annually in Orlando the first week of November and in Kansas City the second week of March.

For more information about either of these national church revitalization conferences or additional resources go to: www.RenovateConference.org.

Twelve Questions to Ask Yourself Before You Select a Model

Before you run full speed into the field of church revitalization and renewal, it would be advisable to consider a few key questions before you anchor your church's future towards a specific church revitalization model. Some of the key preliminary questions to have answered are:

1. What are your particular gifts when it comes to the revitalization of a church?

2. Have you gained a general understanding of the basics required of anyone who would seek to lead a church revitalization effort?[3]

---

[3] For assistance in this area consider the church revitalization primer *Ninety Lessons Learned the Hard Way In Church Revitalization and Renewal* by Tom Cheyney available from RenovateConference.org/bookstore.

3. What adjustments must you make to the model design to help the renewal effort have the best chance for success?

4. What degree of freedom is realistic within this church's renewal framework in order to stretch the church's vision?

5. Are your congregants desiring renewal or mere relief? Will they drop all efforts once the pain of rapid decline is eliminated?

6. Who really are the people you are trying to touch and target for the renewal effort?

7. What human, material and financial resources are still available to the work of church revitalization and renewal?

8. Have you made any unrealistic assumptions due to your passion and

enthusiasm for revitalizing this local church?

9. Have you written down a list of strengths and weaknesses regarding this model and found the strengths outweigh the liabilities?

10. Are there any characteristics within this model that helps the renewal effort or distracts from the church's eventual success?

11. What are the basic suppositions that move this model to the top as a best possible strategy for renewing your specific church?

12. Will this church revitalization model work within the changing community around your present location?

Remember the selection of the right church revitalization model is critical to moving your church towards the best possible success. Though the church renewal effort usually reflects the personality and passion of the church revitalizer as the single solitary leader, proper selection of the model is crucial towards assuring that the church will fit into the culture in which the work is being renewed.

A Quick Rundown of the Diverse Models and Methodologies

A quick rundown of the thirty-eight diverse models or methodologies being utilized in the field of church revitalization and renewal is perhaps the best place to begin. Not all of these models are being used in a wide variety, but they are being used. While I do acknowledge that God does not offer a single magic pill that we all can use, here are actual models being used for the work of church revitalization and renewal. Some of them are often used while others are utilized less frequently. Here is the list of these diverse models:

1. Pastor's 180 Degree Transformation Church Revitalization Model

2. Evangelistic Outreach Church Revitalization Model

3. College Based Church Renewal Model

4. Pioneering Based Church Revitalization Model

5. Disciple-Making Church Revitalization Model

6. Cross-Cultural Based Church Revitalization Model

7. Best-Practices Church Revitalization Model

8. Change Coalition Church Revitalization Model

9. Apprentice or Intern Based Church Revitalization Model

10. Event-Based Church Revitalization Model (Catalytic Event Models)

11. The Missional Sunday School Based Revitalization Model

12. Small Growth Group Revitalization Model

13. Leader Development Church Revitalization Model

14. Preaching Points for Deacons Revitalization Model

15. Utilizing Lay Ministers Revitalization Model

16. Staff Member Based Church Revitalization Model

17. Critical Path Church Revitalization Model

18. Team-Building Church Revitalization Model

19. Leaving a Legacy Church Revitalization Model

20. Associational or Network Based Church Revitalization Model

21. Spiritual Renewal Church Revitalization Model

22. Healthy Church Revitalization Model

23. Church Revival Revitalization Model

24. Where God is Already at Work Church Revitalization Model

25. Relationship Based Church Revitalization Model

26. Restart Based Church Revitalization Model

27. Replanting Church Revitalization Model

28. The High Impact Based Church Revitalization Model

29. Organizational Learning Revitalization Model

30. Program Driven Revitalization Model

31. Portable Church Based Church Revitalization Model

32. Multi-site Church Revitalization Model

33. Church Merger Revitalization Model

34. Affinity Based Church Revitalization Model

35. Mother to Daughter Based Church Revitalization Model

36. Breaking Growth Obstacles Church Revitalization Model

37. Relocation Church Revitalization Model

38. Bi-vocational Church Revitalization Model

As you can see there are many models that range from the very simple to the more complex of models. Some are steeped in the old church growth strategies of the 1970's while others are fresh and new with boldness and vigor.

A few have been tried by the very bold with yet to be determined success or qualitative results. Nevertheless, these are the present models being utilized around the world in the effort to revitalize declining, dying, or deceased churches. In the appendix at the back of this book you will find the *Key Church Revitalization and Renewal Definitions,* which will help you to be aware of the current trends and definitions being utilized within the field of church revitalization and renewal.

Practical advice as you design your individual renewal strategy:

Here are eight practical ideas to consider when it comes to designing your church's individual church renewal strategy. I offer these as guidance worthy for consideration:

- Make your renewal program flexible enough to adjust to the strengths and needs of the emerging new members and existing groups involved.

- Focus on sharing Christ and His purposes for Church renewal.

- Support, rather than restrict, the natural development of church renewal in its own new and culturally developing setting.

- Make church revitalization a large part of the overall program of the church. Give it meaningful representation and empowerment for the work of the kingdom.

- Choose church revitalization models and methodologies that lead to self-supporting renewal efforts that result in spontaneous reproduction and ongoing multiplication.

- Prepare for shifts in immigration patterns when revitalizing multi-ethnic churches. Groups of different socio-economic backgrounds arrive in waves. The strategies for reaching them will vary in every ethnic church renewal effort.

- Make sure the attitudes and perspectives of the mothering agency do not stifle the vision and ownership of the church revitalization effort. If the mother agency holds on to or restricts the effort it may result in dependency. Many mothering agencies are holding on more for their own self-preservation rather than yours.

- Watch out for paternalistic attitudes, which will often surface. These will weaken a group's capacity to establish self-supporting, self-sustaining, and self-propagating churches being revitalized.

Who Do You Call and Where Can You Go?

Alright, you are willing to begin prayerfully to work towards the revitalization or renewal of your local church. You have developed or are about to develop a church revitalization assistance team[4] to assist you in your effort. Is there someone who can assist you with the coaching, mentoring, and journey you are about to take? First check with your denomination's national office and determine if they are doing anything significant in the field of revitalization and renewal. Secondly, if you are open to virtual coaching, enlist the help of a proven organization in the field of church revitalization and renewal via a monthly mentorship of you and your church's core leaders.[5] If you are in an

---

[4] For assistance in this area consider the church revitalization resource *Developing Your Church's Church Revitalization Assistance Team* by Tom Cheyney. Download the resources at: www.RenovateConference.org/resources.

[5] For assistance in this area consider the *Renovate Virtual*

area locally where there is a *Church Revitalization Cohort* already in existence working with multiple churches desiring renewal, ask if you might join the group or the next new one being launched. Another great place to find help is a local church already known for its desire to revitalize churches and ask if the pastor and staff would consider allowing you to intern with them over the next few years while you seek to revitalize your own church. You would be given access to staff, attend weekly staff meetings, be supported in prayer by the church, and held accountable for the things that need to be done by a church willing to officially come alongside of you and your church for the purpose of church renewal. This would be a covenant agreement committed to by both churches and its leadership

Coaching Network led by Drs. Tom Cheyney and John Bailey. Download the application and enlistment information at: www.RenovateConference.org/resources.

teams. A fifth way to seek help is a variation of the last one wherein you ask a cluster of churches and their leadership to help you with the revitalization of your church. This works best when a church is geographically between several churches similar in practice and faith and desire to see that work re-invigorated and become healthy once more.

Three Fears Churches Have Towards Church Revitalization

Churches that have not fully adopted a mindset for church renewal will often experience some fear towards the whole church revitalization endeavor. Both those who are all in for the task of renewal and those who are on the sidelines, unsure if they want to see their church fully revitalized, will have fear about the process. Let's look at some of the most frequent fears faced by church fellowships preparing for revitalization and renewal.

The fear of losing present members if the church begins renewal efforts

There will always be a certain group of church members that will take flight in any church when leadership makes a hard decision to move forward over becoming complacent in the past. Healthy churches as well as unhealthy ones experience this phenomenon, but at different levels. Rapidly declining churches live in fear of new possibilities due to the comfort levels of present members cocooning together in a tightly knit group. Declining churches want growth, but they want growth on their terms which is often the very reason they cannot grow. Things that need to be included in a church's effort towards revitalization are most often the very things the present membership declines to offer.

Granted, those few who are coming are happy with what is being done and how it is being done. Yet, new potential members who could become a viable part of the church's turnaround do not want what the church is presently offering. I concede that there are always fringe church hoppers who will skip to hurting and declining churches in an effort to take over or be allowed a place of leadership, which has been denied them from previous churches they attended. No ethical church revitalizer can renew a church by going after members of other churches as their primary effort towards revitalization. I have found that these types of individuals are not church revitalizers, but people who only seek to build their own kingdom. Some will leave your church as you begin renewal because the effort is too great for those who are complacent and lack the energy to participate in church revitalization and renewal. For those churches and church leaders that are caught in this scenario, the best possible solution for revitalization is to restart the church with a new vision and new leadership.

The fear of having to compete with the many new churches that intentionally target a younger audience

Another large and consuming fear for churches beginning to become involved in church revitalization efforts is the fear of having to compete with the many new churches who intentionally target a younger audience. Struggling churches of decline already feel they are losing their turf to church plants and live in a circle-the-wagons kind of existence. While I would be the first to declare neither church revitalizer nor church planter has the exclusive rights to a particular area. Someone said it well, "Far too many churches compete for Christians, but there is no competition for lost sinners." It is acknowledged that for the church planting community a planter that starts from scratch will usually find 85% of its members coming from the unchurched and most of them will be new believers! This single solitary concept if moved over into church renewal would be perhaps the greatest methodology available to the renewing church. Yet, it is usually the farthest thing from church members and leaders of renewing churches. If your church wants to be revitalized, begin to develop the systems and leaders who are able to bring the lost into your church though various forms of evangelism. After prayer being the foremost initial effort towards revitalization, a compassionate expression of evangelism and outreach into one's community is the best chance you have for church revitalization and renewal. The reason existing churches fear new churches is because they are acknowledging by their practices that they have not stayed in touch with the changing culture of their community and a church planter usually begins there first. The fear that the new church will grow and succeed and get all the glory while the existing church just plods along is a valid fear for churches that have lost the energy for renewal. We often fear that our church will think less of us if another church grows. This likely is personal pride. The blocking of new churches for fear we will not sparkle as brightly is spiritually nauseating.

The fear that our renewal effort will not work and we will be seen as ineffective leaders

Church leaders are human and there is often a fear that the church membership will think less of them if their church renewal effort does not bring about revitalization. While churches are revitalized by the single focus of an unrelenting solitary leader compassioned about bringing about renewal, if laity are not willing to jump in and get involved, nothing positive is going to happen. If lay leadership sits on the sidelines and merely watches, it is not the leader's failure, but the church's failure for allowing lay leadership to thwart the plans of God and His under-shepherd.

It is important that we determine to live by God's grace in a journey of faith and not settle to become comfortable in a field of our fears.

Examination of the Models and Methodologies

Models for church revitalization and renewal come in all forms and sizes. If a group doing the work of revitalization is a larger church, the options for renewal will often be looked at from one of infusion of dollars and new if not more personnel. When a small church is doing all of the work of a revitalization effort it might have a very different look than most. If you are an organization working in the area of church revitalization and renewal, if you are based within a local regional setting then some sort of church revitalization assistance team will usually come alongside of the declining church and assist it in developing its plan and model. National or state agencies tend to suggest models that can be considered from long distances with little or no daily help, such as buyouts and takeovers. Not all of these are bad, but it is important to consider if local help is more preferred over a less personal national effort which seeks to deliver assistance from afar and is less likely to be able to invest the time required for real revitalization of churches. If a preference is desired, the work of local assistance always outlasts the less personal global effort offered by a state or national agency. When I wrote the work *Twenty One Church Planting Models for the Twenty-First Century*, I said that models are illustrations that emerge from pure expressions. I still believe that is true for the field of church revitalization. Models are many and the significant difference behind the diverse models for church revitalization and renewal include:

- Your denominational ecclesiology
- Whether a church or mission organization is doing the revitalization

- The philosophy of the church renewal body

- The theological and spiritual viewpoint of the renewal body

- Factors relating to the context including sociological understanding of the community which the church is being revitalized

- The size of the church revitalization assistance team.

As they relate to church revitalization and renewal, models function as prototypes or patterns. Models offer the church revitalizer or church revitalization coordinators an orientation from which to advance. Missiologist Harvie M. Conn provides a valuable definition: "Models are human, conceptual arrangements of reality, more than abstract theories

6 Harvie M. Conn, "Samples: Linking Strategy to Model," in Planting and Growing Urban Churches: from Dream to Reality, ed. Harvie M. Conn (Grand Rapids, MI: Baker, 1997), 195.

and less than empirical observations."[6] According to

another sociologist, Abraham Kaplan, models provide

exemplifications of "meaningful contexts within which

specific findings can be located as specific details." In

other words, models permit a point of reference to

tangible and observable findings. The observable

findings are compiled into what we term "models" that

function as organized data, relevant characteristics,

criticism or corroboration, imaginative interpretation,

and anticipated or expected outcomes.[7] The models

offer within this work are developed from reality and

understanding and are offered to all prospective church

revitalizers and practicing church revitalizers. Realizing

it is difficult to refine and customize an explanation

appropriate for what is often termed "church

---

[7] Abraham Kaplan, The Conduct of Inquiry: Methodology for Behavioral Science (Louisville, KY: Chandler Publishing Company, 1964; reprint, London: Oxford, 1998), 268-272.

revitalization models," nonetheless these models are offered for consideration.

Pastor's 180 Degree Transformation Church Revitalization Model

Some sort of transformation of the leader leading the local church usually revitalizes churches. One such transformation that is less talked about is when the leader of the local church undergoes such a spiritual transformation that he now has the necessary skill set and energy to revitalize the church and to impact the community for the cause of Christ. One writer has said that most pastors in North America are pastoring churches that will be gone by the year 2100 and many will become extinct long before that![8] When looking to revitalize a church it is vital to see the hand of God

[8] Paul Nixon, *I Refuse to Lead a Dying Church!* Pilgrim Press, 2006. pg. 9.

raise up to the surface a solitary, key, unrelenting and sure leader. The Pastor's 180 Degree Transformation Church Revitalization Model often sees the emergence of a key leader to lead in the revitalization of the local church. The pastor's 180-degree transformation displays to the congregation that they are the one who has a renewed vision and tenacity to see revitalization of the church through to accomplishment! In the scripture individuals such as: Moses, Nehemiah, Gideon, Paul and even Peter were examples of such emergence of a key solitary leader to revitalize a particular state of affairs. Here is the lesson: Churches can and will thrive in vitality when the right individual leader comes into sight! Furthermore, the Lord God will assist present church leaders who are willing to step forward, accept authority, learn key revitalization principles, keep on keeping on, and take responsibility for the health and growth of the church. The initial key for church revitalization in this model is the surfacing of a solitary leader to lead a church through revitalization and into vitality.

The Pastor's 180 Degree Transformation leaders must:

- Seek regeneration over stagnation.

- Choose bold advancement over mild maintenance.

- Desire to be pioneers over patio sitters.

- Decide to move forward now over tomorrow!

- Function more as apostles rather than a lethargic leader.

For the Pastor's 180 Degree Transformation Leader it is essential they have a clear determination to clear new paths and lead the church to new places and reach new people. They must become, if they are not already, personal evangelists and actively participate in reaching individuals for Christ as a personal soul winner. The pastor has a renewed interest in joyfully reproducing disciples. Perhaps, previously there was a fear of taking risks, but now they are not fearful of taking risks for the advancement of the Gospel. Before they were clueless towards prospects and people, but now, suddenly, they are reaching out to new pockets of people not currently being reached in their community. The Pastor's 180 Degree Transformation leader cares more about everyone coming to know Jesus Christ than they care about keeping their churches small enough so that they can know everyone.[9]

Such a 180 Degree Transformation leader needs a new fire, which has been stifled previously.[10] This

---

[9] I have heard this expound by many but not sure who originated this coined phrase!

[10] C.f. Acts 11:16

leader needs a new faith and begins to believe God for something big right now![11] Every 180-degree transformation church revitalization leader needs new fundamentals and skill sets for the task of revitalization. The leaders relearn to trust God for the necessary funds that will be required to revitalize their church. Remember our supply is not in the people we know in our community, but in the Lord God who is our real provider. Ask the Lord to make you such a 180-degree transformation leader and allow Him to bring back life and breath life into your church.

Evangelistic Outreach
Church Revitalization Model

---

[11] C.f. 2 Cor. 5:7; Heb. 11:6.

Utilizing the evangelism approach towards church revitalization and renewal can be argued that it is returning of a declining church back to its original roots of outreach targeted towards the unchurched and unrepentant. It might be said that one reason God "comes" to us for our own salvation is to "send" us on a mission to be instruments of divine grace in the lives of others. In order for this model to be effective, the following things most remain a focus:

- Small church approaches to evangelism need to be person-centered.

- This is the pattern and strength of the small church.

- The small church attracts through the contacts people have with its members.

- Most members in smaller churches believe they are off the hook when it comes to doing evangelism.

- One of the tragedies in many churches today is that no one or very few are involved in evangelism.

As an individual church becomes renewed through a revitalized membership participating in regularly scheduled outreach events, there is a greater effort and opportunity towards a church gaining traction through the new converts and their willingness to participate in new things of outreach and ministry around the church. This model is best fitting for churches recently on the plateau and in areas with a dynamic or dense population base.

College Based Church Renewal Model

The equipping of university students to revitalize local churches utilizing the "simple church" concept from Thom Rainer is a new and helpful model for church revitalization that is focused on using local college students to be semester church revitalizers or multiple semester church revitalizers. Usually this model is accomplished through some type of larger entity, which will fund these semester church revitalizers such as a national convention or state denominational group. All of these models and designs are based around various groups that either have a particular affinity, generational similarity, or ethnic diversity and make up a target grouping.[12] Almost anywhere a university is located, there is a wonderful opportunity for this model to be experienced. Student

---

[12] For an excellent discussion on the subject see *Starting Reproducing Congregations: a guidebook for contextual new church development* by Sanchez, Smith and Watke.

led church revitalization efforts usually focus on the younger populace surrounding a local church situated near a university. The use of students as the primary source for revitalization necessitates that the local pastor be willing to lead this group and work side by side as they assist the pastor in this renewal effort.

There is no single form for renewing of churches within this model since every college campus in North America is different. In the United Kingdom, there are many churches currently being renewed through this methodology by the Anglican Church. Remember that each campus has a unique identity with unique mixtures of ethnicities and socio-economic strata. That said, a one-size-fits-all approach to church revitalization cannot address the variety of contexts found today on North American college campuses. Contextualization needs to be emphasized in these college-based church renewal models. When this term is used, often there are those who believe that these renewal efforts meet on the campus of a particular academic institution. That is far from the typical case. While I must admit that many church plants start that way and seem to struggle to grow past a few hundred, the best thing about this model is that these renewal efforts are not based on campuses, but are located near college campuses so that the manpower necessary for the renewal effort is available. Here are four variations of this model you might want to consider:

- *Church within a Church*

The local church seeks to renew an existing church through adding an entirely new group of participants that meet either at a new time or day at the church. Often this is done by the utilization of a church's gym or its fellowship hall so that a new feel and look might draw others who are not currently being reached thought the present forms of worship.

- *College Student Focused Church*

Sometimes a church in decline will offer a new worship program that targets the college students enrolled at the nearby campus. Someone who is in touch and focused on that age group will usually lead the revitalization effort. Many times, this renewal project will grab the attention of the transitional student and attach him or her to the struggling church because of its effort towards a college or young adult focus. These type of worship experiences mostly meet on Sunday evenings at a little past 8:00 PM and might even last past midnight. One church in the Ohio Valley utilized this strategy to discover three years later that the effort had indeed revitalized the original church through those who were attending the evening experiences and desired the new ministries that the church was now able to offer. It is vital that those working with this method work closely with the governance of the main church in an intentional and collaborative style.

- *Outside the Main Campus Church*

Because there is not a local facility able to house the collegiate-based church revitalization model, sometimes the need to discover a facility outside of the main campus locale will surface. The local church renewal effort is working together with the new worship format and place, but feels it has a better chance for success if it is moved away from the original facility of the renewing church. Many multi-site church renewal efforts have begun this way and then broken off at a later date and become autonomous.

- *International-Focused Church*

This is either a multi-cultural church revitalization effort consisting of a variety of ethnic groups or a mono-cultural church consisting of one ethnic group whose potential was discovered through learning of the cultural shifts in their church community. One characteristic of this church renewal effort is that its attendees are often individuals who are not citizens of the United States and whose time in North America has been limited. They have come for the purpose of education and will usually leave once that has been accomplished. This is a great way to prepare an ongoing ministry, because as some go, others will come and this growing effort is a strong way to revitalize the ministry of the declining church. Granted, it will not look like it does right now, but it will be viable and full of energy, which is something that was lacking before the church began its renewal efforts.

Pioneering-Based Church Revitalization Model

The pioneers of our country were those who were compelled to reach out into the unknown areas of our land and build a settlement that would begin to grow and eventually become a village, a town, or a city. The pioneering-based church revitalization model is where a church revitalizer selects a church that is a prime candidate for church renewal. The church usually does not select them. The individual church revitalizer has discovered something within the particular church community that leads him to believe that there is indeed hope that the church can be restored to a healthy growing community of believers. Often this model starts with a limited number of adherents and a church revitalizer who has his own form of income such as working a job in the community, or a portion of funds is made available through sponsors of the church revitalization project. Once the Church Revitalizer is in place, he begins much like a church planter in building that initial core group of present members and new prospects committed to seeing the church turn around and become healthy and vital once again. As a church planter, we would often use the term "Starting from dirt and dirt only." For the Church Revitalizer, it often has one more thing beyond the dirt and that is a facility (no matter its current state) in which to meet. A Church Revitalizer who utilizes this model must be able to draw the net and gather people via relational and evangelistic skills. Critical to this model is the ability to relaunch fast with a gathering of core group members and assimilation techniques. Strengths to this model include being able to fashion the renewing church's effort according to biblical priorities and community contextualization. The Church Revitalizer is the initiator and catalytic individual serving to gather the talent needed for the renewal work. He either sees an area and begins working early on the revitalization effort, or develops the best-case design or model for an effective re-launch of the church.

Disciple-Making Church Revitalization Model

It was Dawson Trotman in 1955 in a sermon entitled *"Born to Reproduce"*, who challenged all of us working in the discipline of church revitalization and renewal when he said:

> "A passionate call to maturity, spiritual reproduction, and spiritual parenting to help fulfill the Great Commission"

Since that time hundreds of thousands have been challenged by his charge that every believer should experience the impact of God's desire for us to make disciples. Trotman was passionate about three key terms: produce, reproduce, and reproducing of disciples. For the church desiring a turnaround, almost every successful church renewal effort has, to some degree, a deliberate disciple-making effort. This model is not new to the healthy church community since most of us understand that disciple-making is what God intends for His church to do in the same way that Jesus made disciples. Jesus would lead people through sequential phases of spiritual development. These phases are described in different ways by various churches and authors, but the most common element is a commitment to see people grow in Christ from spiritual immaturity to spiritual maturity.

Church leaders of declining churches everywhere are looking for that magic bullet, a new program that can be employed, a pre-packaged activity that they can plug and play. What most pre-packaged programs offer to church leaders is a process and a system for moving people through specific curriculum over a period of time. Many Church Revitalizers have confessed to me that they are more interested in being freed up from having to develop materials and complete systems on their own, so instead they can use less energy as they are just required to teach, give away to another, or facilitate through the material. The leader then can put more energy into other's projects or programs. The result is the leader has developed an organization with many programs so as to appeal to the masses, provided them with something they will enjoy. Pretty soon, however, the leader reaches their capacity and is stuck managing the many programs they have implemented and the members of the organization are stuck, moving like cattle from one program to the next. Stuck churches, which eventually need church revitalization, often have fallen into the pre-packaged plan.

But a church desiring church revitalization and renewal seeking to utilize this model must begin developing disciples one-on-one and challenging those who are discipled to commit to discipling others. Imagine if you, as the leader of your declining church, made the commitment to disciple three people a year? At the end of three years you would have discipled nine fellow labors who could do the exact same. At the end of those three years from your initial efforts of growing believers you would have seen five hundred and twelve people step up and begin discipling others. Also at the end of those three years, if you held true to your commitments, you would have one thousand and twenty-four people who have been discipled. That in and of itself would begin to revitalize any size church. If you held true to your commitment over the next seven years, you would have personally discipled twenty-one individuals which is an incredible church renewal tool! There are a lot of renewing churches today that want to get quick results. They want something that produces an annual yield. The disciple-making model is perhaps the best way. Couple that with starting new groups and you might see the best years in the life of the church before you and not behind you. Jesus made disciples this way and it will work anywhere if the commitments are made to reproduce others.

I believe that making disciple-making disciples should be the work of everyone who knows Christ Jesus. The Great Commission is not simply a suggestion for professional full-time ministers; it is a command for all Christ-followers. None of us are excluded, the priority of our life must be to train other learners of Christ. It starts at the top. It is too easy for church revitalizers to say that they are too busy doing the work of the church to actually be making disciples themselves. They tell others to go make disciples when they are not. Staying busy with ministry "stuff" is just a mask you hide behind so that you don't actually have to cultivate relationships with others where you will model transparency and vulnerability. Relationships are messy and they take time, even unscheduled time.

Our resurrected Lord appeared to His disciples in Matthew 28:19-20 and said:

> *"All authority in heaven and on earth has been given to me. Therefore, go and make disciples of all nations, baptizing them in the name of the Father and of the Son and of the Holy Spirit, and teaching them to obey everything I have commanded you. And surely I will be with you always, to the very end of the age."*

This is known as "The Great Commission" because it was Jesus' final instruction to the Church. This charge displays to the core the heart and DNA of God for His Church. Church Revitalizers would be wise to re-consider this model.

Cross-Cultural Based
Church Revitalization Model

The cross-cultural based church revitalization model is more than a by-product of church work in foreign lands. A successful cross-cultural church revitalization effort will not only impact a new culture through a declining church, it will usually impact the church revitalizer as he learns of ways to impact neighboring communities within a new culture to disciple and send out other church revitalizers who can utilize the same model. This process should become cyclical. The goal of cross-cultural church revitalization then is not about four walls, institution, or creating a safe-haven for worship, but the ability to re-establish a living organism in another culture, for the purpose of spreading the Gospel and building a relational network of supportive churches. These supportive churches should each grow exponentially within their own cell.

The main goal in targeting is to assess an area that is in dire need of hearing the Gospel message. The cross-cultural church revitalizer utilizes targeting as a way to discern where the Lord's work needs to be directed the most, given the revitalizer's wiring and gift set.[13] Every church renewal leader's specific gifts will be to employ and empower, via the Holy Spirit, to better assist the renewal leader in working with new culture. Wherever the revitalizer is discerning to revitalize, much prayer is essential because the sole purpose is being the servant of God, not in edifying

---

[13] For more information go to: www.RenovateConference.org/resources and search for the audio, blog and visual presentation of "*Skill Sets Deemed Necessary in Church Revitalization and Renewal*" by Tom Cheyney.

oneself. Therefore, targeting of the area for renewal must be done with humility, an open mind, and discernment, conjoined with the comprehension of wiring and gifting of those called to the effort.

Best-Practices Church Revitalization Model

Collective IQ is often a great teacher for those working in the field of church revitalization and renewal. Discovering what is working in another's field is a good way to begin to gage what might work in your own. The best practices model for church revitalization and renewal is a method or technique that has consistently shown results superior to those achieved with other means, and that is used as a benchmark for the revitalization of struggling churches. Unusually any form of the best practices model evolves over time and involves various possible improvements a church can make to continue to keep the gospel fresh in one's community and the church active in reaching into its target niche. As various practices are discovered that are working for other churches, one can adapt those that are bringing about positive results in another area. In the field of church revitalization and renewal the term "best practices" is more than a buzzword, but a careful list of techniques which have resulted in turnaround success by other churches facing plateau or rapid decline.

Within this model, Church Revitalization works best when:

- Conflict within the church is non-existent or very low!
- The church is able to handle rising conflict without getting derailed.

- The pastor's ego and control needs are kept in check.

- The church has discovered its identity mission and purpose.

- Worship engages people in praising a living God who is present in the services.

- Laity are working effectively within their spiritual gifts.

- There is a great effort towards developing a connecting community.

- The church believes that their best years are ahead of them and not behind them.

- Denominational distinctions that have formed a movement are embraced.

- There exists the belief that ministry is collaborative.

- It is believed that discipleship is a better choice over the consumer Christian mentality.

- People favorably seek to become deeper and more spiritual over the prevailing decline from spiritual maturity.

- Membership is focused on being true disciples and followers of Christ.

- Church leadership understands change is part of real and lasting revitalization.

- Pastors practice spiritual disciplines daily.

- The church is open to new relationships.

- Secrecy is not part of this new effort, but rather clear communication is.

- God among us is realized and emphasized. He is leading.

- Pastor and people make a good fit!

- The church willingly makes any changes necessary to align it with what it perceives God is calling it to be.

- Prayer is recognized as a necessity for renewal within the congregation.

Best practices are used to maintain a renewed quality and can be based on a church's self-assessment or ongoing benchmarking towards goals and vision. If a church seeks to utilize this model, it is critical that they: develop realistic expectations for the renewal effort, examine the practices other churches are using that are bringing about effective results, breaking free from challenging assumptions which bring about no change, understand that nothing is free and it will take hard work even if you utilize another's best practice, go and observe the best practice in action, be adaptable to the idea and without getting stuck in the mud, understand the church's vulnerabilities if you utilize the best practice, and examine whether your present church structures allow for this practice to have the best possible chance for success.

As a Church Revitalizer, it is wise to not place too much optimism and grandeur about an expected outcome of utilizing a best practice from other churches. Hype will hurt your efforts so walk carefully even though you have seen it work in another place with positive success. If your present practices are becoming ineffective, the implementation of a favorable alternative after you and your leaders have assessed the alternatives may be well worth the risk required to bring about church revitalization and renewal.

Change Coalition Church Revitalization Model

This is often referred to in church revitalization circles as the development of the *Church Revitalization Assistance Team*. Someone has aptly stated, "If you do what you have always done, you will get what you have always gotten." Nothing could be truer in the field of church revitalization and renewal. Many pastors and lay leaders believe that if they work even harder doing the things they are already doing it will lead to church renewal. When a church is ready to realistically face its need for change, some sort of Church Revitalization Assistance Team should be developed within the local church and perhaps assisted by an area church leader for the purpose of developing a new strategy plan for the renewal effort. There are many resources out there and books available which will help a church utilizing the change coalition model for revitalization. Strategy planning usually is a lengthy and tedious process. Declining churches often have difficulty executing strategy plans, often due to poor leadership, inadequate leader support, or lack of unity within the church body.

Every place I go people ask me for a definition of church revitalization. Church Revitalization is a movement within protestant evangelicalism that emphasizes the missional work of turning a plateau or rapidly declining church around and moving it back towards growth. It is led through a Church Revitalization Initiative, which is when a local church begins to work on the renewal of the church with a concerted effort to see the ministry revitalized and the church become healthy. Church Revitalization means that the local church knew how, at one time previously, to renew, revitalize, and re-establish the health and vitality of the ministry. One of the challenges for the laity in the day in which we live is that they have lost the knowledge of church renewal and no longer want to cultivate the skill sets necessary to see their church experience revitalization. Even sadder is when a congregation does not have the corporate memory of a day when the local church was reaching people for Christ Jesus and active as evangelistic witnesses into their community. In the next 15 years, there will be a growing shortage of pastors willing to fill our churches that have low renewal potential. In my denomination, we have 6,000 Southern Baptist Pastors who leave their ministries each year. More than 200 pastors are fired each month. According to one recent article from LifeWay there are 70,000 vacant pulpits in America.

When putting together the local Church Revitalization Assistance Team, always start with players who have the right stuff and then let it push out to the water's edge. You want a team that is quite able, well-led, and displays the right characteristics. Here are some key member characteristics of the local Church Revitalization Assistance Team[14]:

Look for Collaborators

The members must be willing to work together and build the ability to work together as a unified core and not individual MVP's!

Dedication to Church Renewal is Key

Team members must be sold on the idea of revitalizing a church and be fully committed to the task. Placing people on the team will not convince them of the need to renew a work.

Find People with Evangelistic Fervor

[14] A copy of *Determining Your Local Church Revitalization Team* can be downloaded at: www.RenovateConference.org/downloads

To serve effectively on an individual Church Revitalization Assistance Team, members must strongly believe in and practice evangelism. Evangelistic thinkers will have the passion needed to build the Kingdom by renewing churches into healthy bodies once again.

Look for the Optimist not the Pessimist
Church revitalization is a challenging endeavor, so you do not want naysayers on your Church Revitalization Assistance Team. The best type of person to serve on this team are those people who can find the opportunity in every obstacle. They are optimistic about the cause and refuse to fuss and feud over nonessential matters.

People of Faith Make Your Team

The Church Revitalization Assistance Team must be people of faith! They must be willing to believe God for the impossible. They must be able to embrace a vision of what a revitalized church looks like. They must be willing to look beyond what is seen into the unseen. That takes faith.

In addition to the previous-mentioned characteristics, which you will want in every person on the team, there are some additional yet individual specific gifts displayed by various members of the team. It is wise to have at least one of each of these types of individuals on your church revitalization team.

Strategic Thinking

You will need at least one strategic thinker on the team, someone who is adept at reasoning through a process. This person understands goals, objectives, plans, and strategic steps. Strategic thinkers typically ask penetrating questions.

Institutional Memory

This historian-type individual helps the church avoid repeating mistakes. A long-tenured pastor or staff member is such a likely person.

Ministry contribution

People who are active in the church's current ministries will contribute greatly to the team's effectiveness. Determine which groups would be most helpful and involve them as they are needed.

Creative Thinker

Creative thinkers are an asset to the Church Revitalization Assistance Team. Revitalizing a plateaued church is not a traditional endeavor. You will want people who see things a bit off center. These types of team members will stretch the rest of the team. Creative people force others to break free from the confines of conventional wisdom. They help the rest of the team to clearly see new options and think clearly about the choices it makes.

Apprentice or Intern Based Church Revitalization Model

Larger churches working in the field of church revitalization are spearheading this new model for church renewal. While it has been around within the church planting community for a long time, it is now beginning to be utilized to assist a local struggling church faced with the decline of membership and member flight. This model works best when the larger church has built a cohort of churches needing help and a staff member or the local director of missions meets with these leaders monthly to equip them for the work of the revitalization effort. Often these individuals will have a job in the community, but feel the call of God on their lives to go into the pulpit ministry, and the larger church will place them strategically in hurting and declining churches. There are advantages for church revitalization and renewal of a larger church that is developing apprentices for those facing decline. Here are a few:

- **The host church leadership trains the potential apprentices how to be Church Revitalizers**

When a potential church revitalization apprentice takes on the commitment to be coached by those more experienced in church renewal, there is a greater possibility of the church apprentice surviving because of the training and coaching the apprentice has received.

- **The host church is a place where the formation of the apprentice church revitalizer can be achieved.**

Apprentice Church Revitalizers need a place and a space for their revitalization concepts to be worked out as they are in a key environment for learning church revitalization methodologies.

There is a degree of faith required for every revitalizer, but coupled with that is the need to grow in knowledge and practical experience for church renewal.

- **The Church Revitalizer Apprentice will have a lifeline with the host church and a place where a safety net is available so the boldness required for the effort is supported by the pastor and staff of the larger church.**

Since it is difficult to be a church revitalizer, it is critical that the larger church offer a connectedness through weekly or monthly cohorts that focus on assisting the revitalizer with practical helps and coaching.

- **The host church can serve as a wonderful example of the Apprentice**

Church Revitalizer as he continues to learn and grow by having opportunity to be mentored by the lead pastor.

Learning the heart from one who has a tremendous passion for ministry is a great blessing. For an apprentice church revitalizer, it is even more vital, because if they can learn and acquire the necessary church revitalization DNA, they too might join the effort as the host church once they have regrown the work they have been assigned.

- **The host church can often provide financial support for the apprentice church revitalizer for up to three years.**

One of the most helpful things a host church can do is to send out their apprentice church revitalizer with at least three years of funding so the church being revitalized has one less financial challenge as they move towards renewal. This is also a way in which the larger host church can directly assist the weaker church by wrapping its proverbial hands around the church and lovingly directing and encouraging it through the journey.

There are advantages of church revitalization and renewal when a larger church develops apprentices for those facing decline, and yet there are some disadvantages as well. Here are a few disadvantages of a larger church developing church revitalization apprentices:

- **It is difficult for the declining churches to find a larger host church that is willing to take on this revitalization model.**

Not every mega church has a heart for smaller declining churches. Yet there are a growing number of mega churches who do have this heart for the larger Kingdom of God and sister churches.

- **The larger host church will often feel like it is getting sidetracked from its own vision and desire to keep growing.**

This can be a real challenge and yet most of the churches working in the area of multi-site understand that this can be overcome. It is vital that healthy cohorts of four or five apprentice members exist since they will be the glue which will help the host church and the smaller ones the larger church is working with.

- **The larger host church runs out of practical coaching that is fitting to the size of the church being renewed.**

I attended recently a one-day church revitalization conference, which was developed by a local church. It was very light on church revitalization training and teaching and was more focused on what a mega church pastor had done over his long ministry. Since I was in the fellowship hall I was getting text after text from others in the room asking "When will we get to the issue of Church Revitalization?" That was a fair question and sadly even when it was over I had no answer. Here is the point that needs to be understood. A church that gets involved in this effort of training apprentice church revitalizers must either already have the necessary skill sets for mentoring others or be willing to get the skills needed to impart to others. That is why where I serve we have fifteen coaches in training at my monthly revitalization trainings and others who connect through Skype so they can get the skill sets necessary to equip those which they are leading. My favorite little saying about training others across the nation is that as you train others next month in something critical locally, those being trained in another locale really do not need to know that you as a cohort coach had just learned it only three months earlier from one of our Virtual Coaching Network training themselves.[15]

---

[15] For more information go to www.renovateconference.org and under the resources icon connect with the Renovate Virtual Church Revitalization Coaching Network.

- **The Church Revitalization Apprentice might grow more connected with the host church rather than the struggling one.**

Many church revitalization candidates are having so much fun learning what works that they never get to work on the real labor of revitalization.

- **The Church Revitalization Apprentice might become detached from the training due to personal and family issues.**

A Church Revitalization Apprentice must understand that it is a minimum investment of one thousand days if they are going to work with a church through its need for revitalization and renewal. Often these candidates are well-meaning, but lack focus and will begin to stop attending on a regular schedule. When that happens confront the issue right away and either re-challenge or let go. All funding would cease as well unless another apprentice could be inserted into the equation.

- **The Church Revitalization Apprentice wants to depart before the three-year commitment is completed.**

Revitalization takes time so make sure your apprentices understand the investment they are making to the renewal effort and to the host church. Be clear to your staff that these apprentices are not to be bogged down by serving in area of the host church, which would keep them from full focus on the work of revitalization.

Church Revitalization Apprentices are widely used in other forms of ministry and have been around for a long time. While they are initially inexperienced, their greatest asset must be that they are teachable. Because they lack experience it also means they lack most of the bad habits that have killed the target church for renewal. God bless the growing healthy mega church that wants to work in the field of church revitalization and renewal. May their numbers increase as we work all over the world to renew hurting declining churches and reinvigorate them with the passion and compassion Jesus had for lost souls. The time is near and we must be vigilant.

Event-Based Church Revitalization Model

Every church, when faced with either a new launch or an effort to reinvigorate an existing one, has used this model. It is not only a church revitalization model, and yet it is one which often brings about the necessary synergy to begin the process of turnaround. Some churches utilize this model each summer as a means for eliminating the summer slump. Others use this model to attract a specific target group that a church desires to reach. One church revitalizer re-launched his church in our nation's capital using a ten-week approach of events. The danger of this type of model is that you must equal what you experienced when the initial relaunch events are over or flight begins to downsize the work rapidly. Some of the best and most utilized event based models are:

- Seminars

- Niche events

- Youth Rallies

- Concerts

- Children events

- College kickoff events

There are others as well. The key with any form of event-based model is to work toward continuing what has worked or the event will only be an event and you will be back and challenged once more. This model works best in churches with effective and accepted leaders and a good track record of follow-through on decisions and potential prospects.

The Missional Sunday School Based Revitalization Model

The missional Sunday school model is a way for a struggling church to launch a new group in an area which might bring about new growth and be viewed as an outreach effort initially into a community. This model is designed to gather a new crowd and begin a new core so that perhaps eventually a new church would grow out of the effort. By meeting away from the present church's location, those who struggle to visit the local church might feel more comfortable with a less imposing locale.

Small Growth Group
Church Revitalization Model

The Small Growth Group Revitalization Model is a model that can take the stalled church out into the community via groups that are meeting in homes and are open to casting the net towards new prospects and neighbors of host homes. This model is critically important in today's changing cultures. There is a raising gap between what Americans say they believe and what they do. Within the local church the same can be said of believers. Our beliefs do not always transform into actions. Spiritual maturity is often seen in four areas: one's beliefs, one's practices, one's attitudes, and one's lifestyle. These small indicators tell whether an individual has a growing integrated faith, which is transforming each day into closeness with Jesus Christ. Anything less is merely a statement of faith, but not action. As a believer goes deeper from mere belief to consistent lifestyle, the more obvious these four areas will be in their life.

Eric Geiger, co-author of the book *Transformational Groups: Creating a New Scorecard for Groups*, declares:

> Groups are absolutely essential to the health and mission of a church. They are likely the starting point for community, discipleship, and service in your church. In fact, recent research shows that people involved in groups are healthier

spiritually than those who aren't. People in groups read the Bible more, pray more, give more, and serve more. Simply stated: your groups matter.

Ed Stetzer, the other author of *Transformational Groups: Creating a New Scorecard for Groups*, asserts:

> Our research shows that people in a group read the Bible and pray more regularly, confess sins more frequently, share the Gospel more freely, give more generously, and serve more often than those not in a group.

Church Revitalizers, we are the most essential and influential person to launch and continually start small groups and keep the small group ministry alive in our churches. What I have learned is this: The bar I set is the bar my church members will shoot for. Therefore, I must set the bar high when it comes to the making of disciples and small groups. We need to create an attitude of multiplication within our churches and a group is a great way to expand our ministry.

Robby Gallaty, Pastor of Brainerd Baptist Church in Chattanooga, Tennessee says there are five reasons it is better to disciple in groups. The gospels record Jesus ministering in 5 group sizes: the crowd (multitudes), the committed (the 72 in Luke 10), the cell (the twelve disciples), the core (Peter, James, and John), and the close-up encounters (one-on-one). Making disciples cannot be restricted to a particular group meeting; however, a regular gathering time is practically necessary for accountability. While the Bible never prescribes a particular model for discipling others, Jesus invested in groups of varying sizes. Larger groups learned from his teachings and miracles, while his closest followers benefited from personal discipleship and specific instruction.

While one-on-one disciple making is valid and has it purposes, he wants us to consider five reasons to meet in a group of three to five instead of privately with one. Here are his ideas:

1. Avoid the Ping-Pong Match

First, a group of two can be like a Ping-Pong match: you, the leader, are responsible to keep the ball in play. "Mark how was your day?" "Good," responds Mark. The leader probes deeper by asking, "Any insights from your Scripture reading this week?" "I enjoyed it," Mark briefly replies. The conversation progresses only as the mentor engages the mentee. The pressure to lead is lessened when others in the group join in on the spiritual journey.

2. One-on-One can be Challenging to Reproduce

Second, a one-on-one model can be challenging to reproduce because the person in whom you are investing has a tendency to look at you in the same manner that Timothy looked at the Apostle

Paul. Mentees, after a year or two in a discipling relationship, have said to me, "I could never do with another person what you did with me." Yet a group takes a journey together. It is worth noting that group members usually don't feel ready to begin their own groups. Neither did the disciples. But Jesus left them with no choice. Remember, the discipling relationship is not complete until the mentee becomes a mentor, the player becomes a coach.

3. Groups of Two Tend to Become a Counseling Session

Third, a group of two tends to become a counseling session, where you spend the majority of your time solving personal problems. Biblical wisdom for personal issues is certainly a part of the discipling relationship, but therapeutic advice every week must not define the group.

4. Jesus Discipled in Groups

Fourth, as mentioned earlier, Jesus utilized the group model. While he spent time investing in a group of twelve, he used teachable moments to shape three — Peter, James, and John — in a unique way. With the exception of Judas, all twelve faithfully followed the Lord, even to the point of death. But these three were the key leaders in the early years of the church.

5. Built-in Accountability

Finally, a group of three to five provides a built-in accountability system, as well as encouragement from others. In my first D-Group, two of the three men involved came prepared with a Bible-reading journal I had asked them to complete, but one, a skeptic of the system's value, failed to make any entry. Prior to joining the D-Group, his excuse for not reading the Bible was, "It's difficult to understand." Using the other two men to motivate him, I countered, "Can you just try journaling for the next five days? Right now, you have no evidence to prove that it doesn't work. By trying it, you will know if it works for you or not." The next week, he arrived with a smile on his face, saying, "Let me share what I heard from God through his Word this week." Watching the excitement of the others challenged him to contribute to the group, and to his own spiritual development.

Joel Rosenberg and T.E. Koshy pose a thought-

provoking question:

> What if for three years Jesus had discipled only Judas? Despite his best efforts, Jesus would have wound up with no one to carry on his legacy and his message when

he returned to the Father. Jesus didn't invest in just one man. He invested in a group of men from a wide range of backgrounds, including fishermen, a tax collector, and a Zealot (a political revolutionary).[16]

Jesus poured himself into twelve men, and taught us the importance of the group in disciple-making. Yes, there are times when a one-on-one mentoring relationship is beneficial, but in the New Testament, particularly the Gospels, it is not the norm.

Here is a great lesson that everyone working in church revitalization and renewal should consider. There is power in new! The reality is that new groups connect more people than existing groups. Because everyone in the group is new, a new group makes it easier for newcomers to connect than existing groups. For the Church Revitalizer, new groups generate fresh

[16] Joel C. Rosenberg and T. E. Koshy, *The Invested Life* (Carol Stream, IL: Tyndale House Publishers, 2012), 87-88.

excitement and more opportunities for connection and growth in your church. Acceptance in an existing group is often hard as individuals are already well-connected with one another and it is hard to fit in the group. There are open groups and closed groups in most churches regardless of what we call them. An open group is one where new people easily fit in and can begin to develop a connection and do life together. A closed group has been around for some time and there is connection, but it is focused on those who are already part of the group and new prospects find it hard to fit into the group. Rick Howerton, small groups specialist remarks: "most groups become close groups within two years from their conception." He further challenges us when he declares, "they can become missionally stagnant." Launching small groups is a great way to drive growth and revitalization into the work of the church. Start small with two or three new open groups. Branch out as God gives the increase and the workers. Execution of groups will be a key so pay attention to this model and do not relegate it to someone who is not all in about revitalizing your church.

Leader Development
Church Revitalization Model

It is interesting to consider the role that leadership development plays into the field of church revitalization and renewal. There are those who work as a leader developer who believe it is critical to the effort. Yet, if that is really the case, why then are there so many Christian organizations doing leadership training, and yet the health of our churches is at an all-time low? Someone recently remarked to me that there are well over seven hundred Christian leadership groups floating around protestant evangelical groups, and yet if anything, the training of leaders for leadership issues has not actually turned the decline around. While I would suggest teaching about becoming a better leader is important, I am not sure that there is a measure that springs from the effort that says the Church Revitalizer was able to revitalize the church because of what they learned from a leadership trainer. Church Revitalizers need revitalization training specific to the challenges of plateau and decline. Seldom is the issue of leadership learning the key to renewed growth.

But there is one area where this model is vital to the work of revitalization, and that is helping a potential church and church revitalizer know how to pull the trigger towards renewal. Many pastors and lay leaders talk about the need for renewal and yet they spend more time talking than walking through the effort. Successful church revitalizers know when to make the shifts necessary to bring about an opportunity for change and new life. Often in my work with churches and with pastors of declining churches, they have made statements such as: "If only we would have done these things two years earlier before many of the younger members just gave up on us and left the church!"

This is a statement echoed far too many times when it is related to the leader development church revitalization model. Investing in church revitalizers is huge. Helping them to improve as the leader of a renewal effort is massive. But seldom will sending them to a leadership training event be the key ingredient to turning around your individual church. Within my denomination, we have leadership groups tied in closely to a state convention and, while they teach some really good stuff over and over, in the end it is just stuff and not something that will help with church revitalization and renewal.

Here are the eleven top pastor leadership roles laity said were the most important to church revitalization and renewal:

- Visionary (received 1/3 more votes than #2)
- Enabler/Encourager
- Partner/Friend
- Facilitator
- Cheerleader
- Transformational Leader/Change Agent
- Spiritual Leader
- Caregiver
- Manager/Director

- Coach for Success

- Expert/ Initiator

One discovery was the clear difference between pastors who are effective and pastors who are efficient! Efficiency becomes the master of the routine. Effectiveness becomes the master of visionary leadership and the ability to make the hard call.

So, what was high on a pastor's list for church revitalization and renewal? Let's look:

- Know and love your people.

- Preach the Gospel of Jesus.

- Pray and enable your people to pray.

- Help your people reach out to others.

- Help them dream of what they can be for God's glory.

- Work hard; nothing comes easy!

- Accept yourself and your people and press on.

- Be patient; new life grows slowly.

- Hold on to and hold out your vision.

- Celebrate the good that is happening.

- Go ahead and risk new ideas and programs.

- Know and love God.

- Teach God's purpose as found in the Bible.

- Train people in evangelism and church growth.

- Get yourself and others out visiting.

- Take key people with you to training events.

- Start with a committed core; don't wait for everyone!

- Read about and study churches that are growing that are similar in size or just a little bit larger than your church.
- Set goals and move towards a strategic plan.
- Delegate all you can and enlist new people.

The leader development church revitalization model is an excellent strategy for a declining church with a low capacity for change. It is a good model for a church with little or limited resources that can get the help from a mother agency to help them begin the journey towards church revitalization and renewal. Also, for any church that is experiencing the greying of its congregation, development of leaders is an effort that must be taken. Usually the outcome is that the potential pool for these new leaders who could be trained is limited at best, and other models should be considered.

Preaching Points for Deacons
Church Revitalization Model

Wise pastors know the importance of keeping the saints busy with the work of ministry. Nothing could be truer than to keep the deacons of the church involved in the work of ministry instead of in the work of controlling the called and gifted staff. My firm belief is that deacons must be led to be a key outreach arm of the church through evangelism and witness. Any deacon should be actively involved on a weekly basis in knocking on doors and following up on prospects for the local church. On the Lord's Day or other times, it is also a great model to be utilized by the developing of preaching points for the active deacons to preach and minister. This is an area where more work ought to be done. This model utilizes deacons and key lay leaders to form teams from either one church or various churches to begin a preaching point with the desired goal of church revitalization and renewal. Often these efforts pop up in community centers, trailer parks, or other areas that a renewal effort could be started in a low-key way.

The strength of this model for church revitalization is that it is a very inexpensive model to initiate. It is a wonderful way for a church to begin in the effort of revitalizing other churches. What happens over time is that these preaching points transition over to the leader leading of the renewal effort who may ultimately become the Church Revitalizer of the effort towards revitalization. It is my firm belief that denominations and state conventions should be doing more towards this in the future. If it could be anchored though a local organization with boots on the ground such as a local church or association, this would be a tremendous help in developing future healthy churches. By moving the leaders of these preaching points towards becoming the Church Revitalizer, the question of responsibility of who is leading dissolves and the leader naturally takes ownership of the church's renewal efforts in the future. Any issues that were murky are now clearer since there is one leading the effort of renewal for the declining church.

Utilizing Lay Ministers
Church Revitalization Model

With the rise of missional living all around us, this method, which surfaced in the early 1960's, is beginning to be practiced again with good results. Pastors are raising up potential church revitalizers from their membership ranks and deploying them for the work of renewal in many places. While this model was initially used by many churches for church planting purposes, I have always been excited to see lay people get involved in the revitalization of churches. A great way to begin utilizing this revitalization model using lay ministers is to gather a group of laity who desire to see churches revitalized and then pair them up and send them out, but keep them connected to the sending church for training in the areas of revitalization they will need.

In the Book of Acts, we see seven laymen from one congregation begin to assist in the work of ministry (Acts 4:13). Many protestant denominations and local churches owe their past growth in a large measure to the historical emphasis on lay involvement. It was through the use of laymen to start Bible classes and

Sunday Schools that we experienced our largest growth! The model will still work for today's church revitalization, I might add.

Staff Member Based
Church Revitalization Model

Effective Ministers of Missions in larger churches have found that hiving off of a core group from the mother church is an excellent way to launch a new work. The same can be said for church renewal. This is more than sending two couples to lead the revitalization team, but a complete core group committed and ready to begin the work of church revitalization and to function as the nucleus of the renewal effort. One example is in South Georgia where a renewal team held meetings on Sunday evenings for almost a year in order to learn how to do the work of revitalization. During this time, they met with the local area superintendent. After that initial year of training, they branched out to begin the work of revitalizing a local church in a rural community not more than ten miles from the staff member's church. The result was that the church needing renewal was blessed by the pastor and staff of a growing church, which allowed the staff time to work with the declining church each Sunday evening. After the initial three-year effort, the declining church became healthy again, with 215 people now calling it their church home each week. The staff returned to the mother church as a search committee called two staff members to lead the church into the future.

Critical Path Church Revitalization Model

There is a model being developed by some that has been labeled the critical path church revitalization model. It is a model that places a huge emphasis on the research that can be discovered before a declining church is selected as a candidate for revitalization. It is a model some are not wired to consider, yet if you only have a specific amount of time, resources, and talents for the renewal effort, selecting the best candidate from declining churches is a good idea. Researchers such as LifeWay Research have documented what revitalizing churches have been doing. This research can then be used to establish a critical path for revitalization. It is interesting that about ten years ago there were three hundred churches specifically selected and analyzed in regards to their church revitalization efforts and success. In 2010, these churches were researched only after seven years of turnaround. Some were still healthy examples, but most were not.

Making a wise selection of a church you want to work with is critical. Not every church is ready for revitalization and despite what they say in relation to the need for renewal, unless they place high priority on a willingness to change, they are not the best candidates for you at this point in time. Use your research to help decide if the church is a viable candidate or not.

Team-Building Church Revitalization Model

The Team-Building Church Revitalization Model is one which many churches and church revitalizers are finding helpful. It is a team of individuals working together to restore a previously healthy church back to new life. The two primary reasons for developing a team approach for church revitalization are:

- The importance of team ministry to assist in revitalization
- The benefits of team ministry to support revitalization and renewal

When you consider the New Testament and look at the ministry that was accomplished, you quickly realize that ministry was being done in teams. Jesus ministered through a team of disciples,[17] the Apostle Paul ministered through a team which initially consisted of Him and Barnabas.[18] Later, for their first

---

[17] C.f. Mark 6:7.

journey to plant churches, they enhanced the team by adding Mark.[19] As Paul began his second excursion to plant churches he then added Silas,[20] Timothy and Luke,[21] and he even added others which we do not know by name.[22]

There are benefits for doing church revitalization as a team:

- A church revitalization team brings together numerous individuals with various gifts, talents, and abilities.

- A church revitalization team is a way to accomplish more than an individual church revitalizer can accomplish.

---

[18] C.f. Acts 11:22-30.

[19] C.f. Acts 13:2-3,5.

[20] C.f. Acts 15:40.

[21] C.f. Acts 16.

[22] C.f. Acts 18.

- A church revitalization team can minister to one another as the needs become challenging and the work becomes hard.

- A church revitalization team can help the Church Revitalizer keep your church on track.

Leading a church through church revitalization and renewal becomes impossible when the church's leadership is unclear about the actual mission and vision of the church. At the opposite end of the spectrum, the church working towards revitalization is dramatically increased and empowered when a majority of the church members join the leadership in pursuing the mission or vision of the church. It is vital to realize as a revitalization pastor working in renewal that you are not in the leadership role to police the petty squabbles that take place at church! As a revitalization leader, you are there to keep the church on course, understanding and sensing from the Lord God that you are doing what He has called you to do in reaching those who need Christ and then providing a way for these new believers to become fully functioning followers of Christ!

Bringing about church revitalization is not easy, but we must be extremely careful not to make it more complex than it needs to be! Utilization of the team model for revitalization can help. Someone must lead the church! It is better if you as the pastor take on that task. Your laity must be able to see clearly where the church is and should be going. You must be the visionary leader who hears from the Lord God and shares it with your people. If you choose not to hear and then share what God is telling you, your people will have an unclear and unstable view of the future under your leadership. Chaos becomes the eventual norm instead of a vision that people can buy in to. Keep your people working with you in developing a vision and watch a greater number of participants follow willingly and joyfully towards a healthy future. It is much wiser to get moving in revitalization than spending large number of hours trying to define what church revitalization actually looks like. Let the revitalization process shape you. If all you do as a pastor is fix problems you will not get very far in ministry. Real ministry will be sacrificed for status quo encouragement. The result will be that church revitalization will not have much of a chance to succeed if that is the form and function of your church's ministry.

In most churches needing revitalization this approach would require some form of restructuring, but this model is well-suited for a church that has an adequate, but ineffective team or committee structure. This approach is also great for a smaller, deacon-led church.

Leaving a Legacy Revitalization Model

Some churches wait too long before they consider working in the area of church revitalization and renewal. Once critical mass has been lost and has dwindled to below fifty adult active members it is very difficult to develop the necessary momentum needed to begin the process of revitalization. When this happens usually one of two things will occur. The first is that the church will become angry and look for someone to blame while wanting to hang on a little longer in hope of a miracle. Those stiff backs stand up and defy someone to help them unless they do it their way, which currently is clearly not working. The other thing that may occur is to deed the church facilities to an association that can put either church planters or a church revitalizer in place.

It is a best practice to close the church and deed the property over to the association service, which allows for a dignified closure and transition from rapidly declining church to new church revitalization effort. There are some groups, however, that will place a church planter in the mix and want you to deed your facilities over to a national agency, which just might later sell it to recoup its cost of investing in your church for three years. The preferred choice is giving it to the local association, which can place multiple plants and restarts into the property and therefore leave a legacy for the former church. One such church in Orlando had declined to about sixteen people. It gave the facilities over to the local association and today it is known as the Rosemont Outreach Center with three churches meeting weekly in the facilities and around two hundred people now on campus each week.

Does your church need to consider and recognize that the existing ministry is approaching an end? This is a procedure that will allow you to start down a new path of church revitalization and renewal to create a lasting impact and reach your changing community. This Leaving a Legacy Church Revitalization Model may be the very next step for your church to consider.

What looks to be a crisis can really be an opportunity provided by God to allow your church to do something glorious for the Kingdom of God.[23]

Here is a brief synopsis of the Leaving a Legacy Church Revitalization Model and its conditions:

- To be considered for a Leaving a Legacy Church Revitalization model the local church will allow

---

[23] If you have come to the realization that it is time to consider a restart for your church, we have a plan and want to talk with you about a process for planting a new church right in your community. To explore this Leaving a Legacy Church Revitalization Model, contact Dr. Tom Cheyney, Founder & Directional Leader of Renovate National Church Revitalization Group at tom@renovateconference.org or legacy@renovateconference.org.

a Church On-Site Assessment to be conducted in order to determine the feasibility of such an agreement.

- The potential Leaving a Legacy Church will agree to a change in leadership and decision-making makeup.

- The Leaving a Legacy Church will approve by vote of the church in an officially-called business meeting to deed over all properties and assets to an Association or church revitalization network for the purpose of placing a Church Revitalizer into the revitalization project.

- The Leaving a Legacy Church Revitalization model will call for the local church to allow the revitalization association or network to develop a Church Revitalization Assistance Team which will work side by side the Church Revitalizer for the purpose of support and counsel during the revitalization project.

This model is in most cases a last-ditch effort to allow the church an opportunity to seek revitalization and renewal before it collapses and looses its ability to maintain critical mass. Many a church simply waits until it is too late and then can only use this model for an effort of revitalization. If you and your church are in this state of rapid decline, please take the time to contact us at the Renovate Group[24] and allow us to come along side of you for the purpose of leaving a legacy for the Lord through the effort of restarting your church fresh and a new.

Association or Network Based

[24] To contact Dr. Tom Cheyney, Founder & Directional Leader of Renovate National Church Revitalization Group at tom@renovateconference.org.

Church Revitalization Model

The Association or Network Based Church Revitalization Model is one that is quickly taking hold across North America since the most logical group to assist in the work of revitalization is the local boots on the ground network. In a day where larger entities, far removed from the local work, are vying for control of these churches, it is a wiser choice to allow the local association or network to be the one that comes alongside and works with the local church to bring about renewal. There must some someone who will coach, guide, and assist the local declining church. It cannot be done weekly from a national denominational office. Nor can it be done from a state denomination office that is merely seeking to try to remain viable in a day where most question the need for their existence.

When a church gets in trouble it is better to have a local individual who is aware of the changing cultures and shifts happening in a selected area then to call someone who sits far away and does not think, pray and help the dying church everyday. The local association can help assist churches who have a desire to revitalize the work of the local church better than any other organization.

The local association can set up a task force to work along side of the struggling church and present options, tools, and techniques that could be utilized in the work of renewal for the church. Your local Director of Missions or Missions Strategist should be well-versed in the skills sets necessary for a church and a church revitalizer to turn around a church. Selecting those who are local boots on the ground missionaries is the way to work rather than the further away not connected larger entities.

Spiritual Renewal Church Revitalization Model

Nothing can turnaround a church in rapid decline faster than a healthy dose of Holy Spirit empowered transformation! For the church utilizing this model, while we can never force the Holy Spirit to do our bidding. When we align our lives back under His control and seek the Lord's deliverance, much can happen way beyond our control. God wants to see our churches stay healthy and get back to health. When God's people humble themselves, repent of their sins, and kneel under the guidance of the Lord, this model is a wonderful demonstration of the power available for the local church. A power which we have often forgotten or have created such an obstruction so that we were unable to receive such blessings.

Here are a few of the ingredients necessary to allow the Holy Spirit to re-invigorate a church:

- Individual repentance

- Corporate repentance

- Prayer becomes paramount

- Movement only as God begins to show His blessings

- Not getting out in front of God as had happened in the past

- Pockets of groups all across the church praying for church revitalization

- Lay leaders demonstrating reliance on God

- Staff demonstrating a renewed commitment towards spiritual things.

Healthy Church Revitalization Model

As a church begins to learn about how the Lord would have a church regrow, there is a health quotient that begins to surface. There are a large number of resources available for this model such as: Becoming a Healthy Church (Macchia); Natural Church Development (Schwarz); and Twelve Keys to an Effective Church (Callahan). Most of these resources are built upon some type of church health assessment and have been developed over years of research with individual churches. For the healthy church revitalization model, churches must look at their journey over no less than five years, but possibly as long as fifteen years. What are the things the church does well and those things the church must improve upon? An analysis of strengths and challenges is usually the first place to begin. This model builds upon refining the things that are working in the church while eliminating those items that are not helping the church move towards growth. While this is often one of the models many churches consider initially, it is a model which is still in question since the "bigger is better" church growth movement of the 1970's and 1980's left so many with little success and little results. To be fair to that old movement, part of the challenge was that the majority of churches considered themselves a whole lot healthier than they really were. Because of this fondness of themselves and the mirror on the wall syndrome, most churches do not have a clue about what to do to lead the church back towards health. That weakness is a crippling one which must be turned around through a greater effort of working together collaboratively to see churches come back to health.

My friend and former work associate Greg Pena, who is a church revitalizer in Oklahoma, and I suggest that there are some critical benchmarks that should be considered when it comes to this church health model for revitalization and renewal:

- **Divine Enablement**

  The healthy church revitalization model recognizes God's sovereign role in building the kingdom and joyfully seeks and expects His Holy Spirit's work in and through the Body of Christ.

- **Competent Pastoral Leadership**

  The ministry of church revitalization must have a competent Church Revitalizer leading the charge. He is un-relenting in the effort toward bringing about renewal. The healthy church is led by a pastor who demonstrates the calling, character, and competence to help this church achieve its God-given purpose and shared vision. Many churches today are discovering that though a pastor can preach, good preaching may not be enough to turnaround a local church. It takes tunnel vision for a new goal. It requires a leader who works diligently to build systems that will give the church the greatest chance for renewal, and a leader who knows how to build a new consensus focused on revitalization of the existing church.

- **Christ Exalting Worship**

The healthy church magnifies Christ by providing worship experiences that engage the whole person and lead the congregation into God's presence.

- **Effective Forms and Tools for Evangelism**

This model necessitates a systematic approach towards evangelism which many churches today are discarding. In a day where many churches are eliminating any and all forms of evangelism, either personal or mass, a church in decline must return to the Gospel witness and the work of being personal soul winners. The healthy church embraces its mandate to multiply followers of Jesus Christ and more healthy churches.

- **Ministries of Compassion**

The healthy church actively expresses the love of Christ through generosity and service to those in need.

- **Developing a Loving and Caring Community**

The healthy church practices genuine care for one another while embracing new people and valuing their inclusion in the fellowship.[25] Many are hurting in our day and the building of loving groups and church systems is a wonderful way to reach out to a new

---

[25] C.f. Ephesians 4:32.

group of individuals which need Christ and the local church.

- **A Growing and Maturing Faith**

The healthy church nurtures spiritual maturity that shapes Biblical beliefs and transforms behaviors consistent with a holy life!

- **People Involved in Various Types of Personal Ministries**

God never said that as saints we had to do everything possible to fulfill our spiritual gifts He gave us. He said we must utilize our gifts towards the work of ministry. It is vital that the rank and file of most local churches re-learn the necessity of doing ministry as a believer. So many want someone else to do it so nobody does it and nothing gets done. The healthy church expects and equips its members to discover, develop, and use their gifts for fruitful ministry. If we begin to emphasize that everyone in the church is a minister and that we each need a ministry in which to participate, as we utilize our God given gifts the Lord can turn the church around towards renewal and revitalization.

- **Development of New Leaders and Strengthening all Forms of Leadership**

The healthy church identifies those who could become new leaders. It also trains and retrains existing levels of leadership. The model empowers individuals who are called and gifted for servant leadership.[26]

- **A God-honoring Biblical Model for Stewardship**

---

[26] C.f. 2 Timothy 2:2.

Far too many believers lack the commitment today to practice biblical stewardship. This is one of the reasons the local church begins to stall and become stagnate as a viable means for reaching the lost. Churches that will not emphasize and people who will not practice biblical stewardship is a sure sign of a declining church headed towards either a plateau or rapid decline. I have had many pastors tell me that they cannot preach on stewardship. My response to them is usually to ask the question if they have troubles with being a faithful and regular tither to their own church.

I had a pastor ask me to come in and do an assessment with the church's key leader and staff. During that time together we discovered that less than four percent of its present membership actually were tithers. As I worked towards ways to overcome this challenge, in private the pastor stated that he did not tithe in a regular fashion. I asked him how he thought that was right and his response was so unbiblical it shocked me. He said because he gave of his time so much that equaled out and he was not required to tithe of his income. I replied he was blatantly wrong and that he might be the reason God has chosen to not bless his church renewal efforts. What further surprised me is that during the next few weeks five of his members who were present at that meeting told me they knew the pastor did not tithe so why should they. The healthy church teaches and practices Biblical stewardship and provides opportunities for generosity in time, talents, and treasures.[27]

---

[27] C.f. Malachi 3:10.

- **Development of an Outreach Focus Church**

The local church must learn how to come out of its walls and begin to embrace the community. There are so many myths exposed by leaders of churches who have given up on any significant growth potential working in a community that even a few shared myths would flow into too many for illustration. Many believe that as a community decreases, so will a church decrease. That is perhaps for many an excuse for developing a maintenance mentality, which will lead to church decline, and a poor view of the miracles available to praying people for God to do a great work again!

Here are some points to ponder in the midst of any church getting serious about Church Renewal or Revitalization:

- People are still hungry for a meaningful sense of community and belonging!

Churches that provide a meaningful sense of community usually connect with their communities and are often filled on Sundays. The need for social connections are always being revised and churches need to continually be aware of these revisions. Things like Facebook and Twitter are ways many are finding to network socially.

- Very few will remain loyal to any church or organization unless they perceive that it is working for them! Choices relating to church loyalty are a part of the church today. Boring church experiences or a lack of relevance will not be tolerated. New generations look at church in a different light. What was a draw thirty years ago is not a draw today. While the Word of God will not be returned void, your expression might be. So, take a serious look and determine if you are reaching those who need to be reached.

- Growing thriving churches seek to pour themselves out into the community through acts of service.

- The desire is to see their membership live Christ out beyond the walls of the sanctuary! Choosing community over isolation means thinking community more than thinking what we need or want. It translates into embracing your community in all that you do. The most effective revitalization pastors turn off their computers and get out into the community so they can spend meaningful time each and every day to interact intentionally with those within their communities.

Have you stopped to consider that perhaps the people who are dropping out and leaving your church are not leaving it because they do not want community, but because they think they have a better chance to find it somewhere else? Here are some helpful possibilities for community connections:

1. Clean-up after large community events.

2. Offer to serve as a mentor or reader in the local school system.

3. Street washing.

4. Service projects that attract the lost to work along side the church.

5. Offer to utilize a specific skill to assist as a volunteer in school. Things like announcing

games, coaching the debate team or science team.

6. Paint play ground equipment in a community.

7. Smaller Ball Parks refurbished. Lawns cut!

8. Offer to serve as a volunteer chaplain for the fire department or police department.

9. Offer your services to funeral directors to be on call if they need a pastor to minister to families who do not have a minister or church.

10. Begin hanging out at the local fitness club so you can develop conversations with those who get to know you.

11. Do the same thing at your local coffee house where a connection might be made.

12. Offer your church's facilities to smaller groups or sporting teams for banquets. Many of the non-profit teams have no funds to secure a banquet place so your offer will be appreciated.

13. Host a repair Saturday where you assist single mothers and singles with minor car repairs and oil changes.

14. Offer ESL classes for those who need to learn English in your community.

15. Select a day once a year where the church moves out into the community on a Sunday and does acts of kindness instead of gathering in a building for worship.

Vision-Directed Systems

The healthy church has its varied ministries focused and working together around the central purpose of fulfilling its vision. If you choose community as a church, often you will discover that they will begin to choose you and your church! Take a page from the church planter's handbook: Devote much energy to community building and it will help you grow a new church. Fail to devote such time and it will help you to kill one! Remember: If you and your church choose community a large portion of time will need to be spent in praying for new group leaders, recruiting new group leaders, and training new group leaders. Church planters know this and the church revitalization pastor of an existing church would do well to understand this also. The healthy church reaches into its community and the world as compassionate, culturally responsive, disciple-making ambassadors of Jesus Christ.

Church Revival Revitalization Model

Not every church can be revitalized through an old fashion church revival. But some can! Without substantive change, results of renewal may be short-lived as old problems may return. Evangelistic preaching focused on those who have not placed their faith in Jesus Christ as Savior and Lord is still a model that works in revitalization of churches. Yet most churches that are stuck in decline are fearful of trying this model. These churches and church leaders have lost the faith necessary to see a great move of God's work in a community and in a church's life. God still does reach unrepentant souls with the gospel message. If a church's leadership and its membership really desire to see people come to saving faith and will work hard at getting friends, relatives and neighbors to such a revival meeting, God will and can do His part. A local congregation can experience spiritual renewal through revival meetings, solemn assemblies, and a renewed prayer emphasis. It is acknowledged that to many a degree an atmosphere of revival enhances all of these church revitalization models within this book.

Where God is Already at Work Church Revitalization Model

I prefer to call this the Blackaby Model for Church Revitalization personally because of my deep appreciation to Henry Blackaby. While I worked at the North American Mission Board, Blackaby took the time to mentor and coach our church planting group team periodically in his office on the south end of Atlanta. It is a better description the larger name given, yet it was Henry's tremendous work *Experiencing God* which taught many of us to get in on where God was already at work and watch His abundant provisions. This model is built upon three books all written by Blackaby, and they are:

1. Experiencing God
2. Experiencing God Together
3. Fresh Encounter

Many a church has initially begun its efforts towards church revitalization through the utilization of these wonderful materials. This is a great model for the smaller and very small church working to turnaround a local church. Large group leading would work best in a smaller church and building a coalition towards renewal that is united towards that aim.

Relationship Based
Church Revitalization Model

The relationship-based church revitalization model descends from the development of its renewal core effort through building of new connections and the re-strengthening existing relationships. Select any single church as an example and you will quickly understand that, to a degree, all churches are relational. The oikos nature of any church is formed upon and continues to be built upon by the regular gathering of individuals into a group that develops relationships. All throughout the scripture we see the example of relationships.

So, what makes this form of church revitalization different from any of the other models for church revitalization and renewal? It is designed from the initial concept for renewal as one that highly values the journey of doing life together and the development of deep as well as wider relationships. This model is all about group connectedness and group cohesiveness. External structures such as programming, where you meet, core purposes, or personalities have little or no initial impact in the development of this model for church renewal. The term *Relationship Based Church Revitalization Model*, is used to define any kind of revitalization effort that is based on relationships and is often utilized as a descriptor for smaller church revitalization emphasizes where there is loose structure and very fluid organizational designs. Some of the most common of these would include, but not be limited to:

- Remnant revitalization efforts which meet in homes

These church renewal efforts happen when a church has fallen to almost nothing and a catalytic church revitalizer takes church planting theory and begins with a relaunch. This relaunch begins meeting in someone's home because there is only a tiny remnant left, possibly due to the church's failure to adapt to the changing culture of the community around the church. This failure caused most members to take flight. In some situations, there was a hostile takeover of a church (c.f. Steeple Jacking) by a mega church and a small group is left due to the struggle of the hostel takeover.[28]

- Revitalization efforts which meet in Café's

There are revitalization efforts where the church revitalizer leaves a church because of its unwillingness to make the necessary changes required to reach out to the lost and unchurched. This is happening more and more as ministers are developing other forms of income and refuse to lead a dying church that is unwilling to change with the times and make shifts in order to continue to be viable for the work of ministry.

---

[28] For more information regarding the *Dangers of Steeple Jacking* go to www.renovateconference.com/resources and download the *Dangers of Steeple Jacking* resource guide, PowerPoint, and audio recording.

The challenge of these relationally-based renewal efforts is that they are often organized around a high value on both community and evangelism, but not necessarily church reproduction or mission to the world. Usually while these groups are in the formation phase of the beginning renewal effort there is a low commitment to thinking about larger issues for the church, such as becoming a sending church and beginning the journey of becoming a multiplying church. Churches that are becoming revitalized make great potential sponsors for new works since they are very in tune with changing cultures and new viable ways to reach people and groups.

The strength of this form of renewal effort is that it is easily reproducible at every level. Because there is little or no baggage, this model can move quickly because there are not a lot of burdens holding them down. Some of the burdens many churches encounter in their attempt to seek church revitalization and renewal are:

- Church facilities that hinder growth because of cost of upkeep.

The church struggles to do ministry because it spends what little resources it has on upkeep and preservation of antiquated buildings. Further, because churches facing the need for church renewal are often challenged with a changing community around their facility, the limited mobility makes the church permanently anchored and unable to relocate should the need arise. Monies that need to be used for church renewal and outreach are strapping the church as it maintains a building it no longer needs or can afford. Renewal efforts must focus on going-and-telling over the come-and-hear mentality of proclamation.

The Restart Based Church Revitalization Model

The restart based church revitalization model is being used all across North America. Any group planting churches or working in the area of church revitalization should have a restart strategy if it is going to be a wise steward. I never sought to write a step-by-step process for doing a church restart.[29] Yet, so many have used this material over the last twenty years that it has become just such a process. I initially learned most of my first efforts, now over twenty years ago, in this endeavor from Ralph Hodges' work and then it just kept growing. Sometimes I get kind notes of encouragement thanking me for the bold stance and unwavering advice offered within the larger set of

---

[29] For more information on the Restart Church Revitalization Model go to: www.renovateconference.org/resources and download the new book by Tom Cheyney and John Mark Clifton.

materials that support this model. A few times I have been ripped apart by those not brave enough to consider such drastic steps to move their local church towards a new expression of health and vitality! The idea of a church that is dying taking the necessary steps to provide it the best chance for survival is not an easy idea to consider. For those who have been part of the setback, admitting that they have hurt the church is hard indeed. Those who will take over also have a challenge in that it will be under their watch that they seek to change those traits, now embedded in the local church, for the betterment and opportunity to turnaround a church that is in rapid decline.

It is amazing to me today that many individuals that attend a dying church see nothing wrong biblically with allowing their church to die along with them. It is as if there is a secret message, which reads: "The last one alive, remember to turn the lights out!" Humorous? Possibly! Tragic for sure because the local church is the very thing for which Christ Jesus gave His life, and yet we treat His local church with such irreverence sometimes, that it is no wonder churches are dying all across the world. If the two disciplines of church revitalization and church planting could join forces at this point, perhaps it will be the local church that wins. Change is going to happen within the small rapidly declining church and this strategy offers an opportunity for a turnaround that is working, has been working for decades, and needs to be reconsidered in light of the advancing decline and plateauing of our churches today.

Not Every Church is a Candidate for a Restart

Interestingly, many laymen often ask me if I think that their church could be a candidate for a restart. Usually they share of the need for their church to be revitalized. A serious of questions frequently follows, of which I will answer each and every single one. Once they wear out in asking questions, I ask one. That question is: *"How willing are you and your lay leadership to let go of the controls of the church for the next three years and allow someone else to make the decisions necessary to restart your church?"* One of two things happen at this point.

No Need to Bleed

The first response is that the individual and his co-leaders see no need to make such a drastic decision. There is no real need to make those necessary decisions that will stop the bleeding of the exodus. After all they have been leading the church for over twenty years and see no reason to make this change despite the decline they are facing. Failure to admit one's weakness and need for a restart is often the initial response. Their emphasis on former glories over present or future glories is a key to the polarization and stuckness they face. As a layperson, you have more to do with the church in its present state then you often take credit. Whether the congregation in which you belong is thriving or declining, it is ultimately up to you and your fellow members and because of you and your fellow members. Pastors are called to equip the saints for the work of the ministry and they can teach, encourage, train, lead, and inspire! But when the rubber meets the road, your church's health is a function of how you and your fellow members relate to one another, to the community in which the church is located, and to how you respond to God's leading within their lives.

John 10:10 reminds us that Jesus said:

"I came that you might have life, and have it abundantly."

We need to be reminded that as laymen we are the church!

Is There a Guide to Stop the Slide?

The other response is less common, but occurs when the leader asks how this could happen and who would assist them in considering such an option. The question was once asked this way, *"Pastor is there a guide we can follow in order to stop the slide we are facing?"* Some laymen desire to stop the near death throws of their dying church and take the drastic steps necessary to help it become healthy and vibrant once more. They are more concerned about the future needs by allowing the Lord to bring about a resurrection of life the way God wants over that with which man has become comfortable.

There is a guide to stop the slide and it is found in the Bible. When a church has allowed a deep state of slumber to creep into the work and ministry of the local church, it is challenging to make the changes necessary for revitalization. Here are ten reasons:

- All around us the world has changed, but the local church has lagged behind these changes and fallen far behind.

- Our world is growing every day and the local church in decline is purging itself at an alarming pace.

- The world embraces the young, but in declining churches the young are feared.

- The younger generations are returning to church, but the rapidly declining church sits on the cliff of fatality refusing to change to embrace this new church attender.

- In the rapidly declining church there is a void of young individuals in the populace.

- The young are in minute numbers, the middle-aged worker is absent, young families are few, and the late middle-aged and older individual are many.

- Older members are in disgust about what younger people want in worship, while the younger individual looks at the older as irrelevant.

- The rapidly declining church is unable to keep up numerically, financially, spiritually, and physically.

- The local expression of church has allowed deadness, un-resuscitated, lifeless form to exist without an attempt to turn the expression around.
- The world sees a need for change in the local church, yet those within have become so comfortable that they miss the need of the lost world for it to remain relevant.

When we are talking about a true "church revitalization restart," I am not referring to the typical small, struggling church that finds fresh life and growth, nor am I looking at mergers or relocation of existing churches. A church that is a candidate for a church revitalization restart has already sought advice from the local association leader or district leader about disbanding or is almost ready to disbanded. The church has dwindled down to about twenty or thirty survivors who are too tired to continue on. They no longer possess the critical mass necessary to get the church healthy once more. The leadership which remains, is too tired, too ineffective, and too small in numbers to bring about the changes it will take to make the turn. Those who are left are at the end of their rope and often want to make decisions that are unwise or lack any chance of success.

What Kind of Church is a Good Candidate for Revitalization Using the Restart Strategy?

There are some churches that have a better chance of living again through a restart. Five types are most often found:

*The Church has no debt and few bills

*The Church is still in a strategic location for a work

*The Church, if it is not the first two, might want to sell property and use the money through the local association to fund a new church plant.

*The Church, if it sells the building, might offer it at a reduced rate to a new church plant so both sides win and Jesus is honored.

*The Church might be used for a new group of people previously not ministered too.

By utilizing this model, not only do we regain a vital testimony for the gospel which had been lost for some time, but we also eliminate the meager witness that was there previously.

Replanting Church Revitalization Model

While the replanting strategy is similar to the restart strategy, the big difference is that this model is seeking to start a new congregation or multiple congregations utilizing the present facility of the former church. Usually, this looks like some form of the following:

- One main plant meeting at the primary service times of Sunday morning

- One smaller church plant which might be an ethnic or language launch meeting in the early afternoon for most of the afternoon.

- One other middle size plant utilizing the facilities from late afternoon through the evening.

The Replanting Church Revitalization Model enables us to salvage and rescue valuable resources for gospel purposes. Millions of dollars have been invested in land, buildings, and equipment as faithful believers have given over many years. In dying churches these resources are being applied poorly. Church planters are often anxious for land and facilities of their own; often their best people must set up for weekly services in rented schools, warehouses, or hotel ballrooms. Rescuing aging churches which are on life support at best, may in many situations, be a good stewardship usage. If believers do not revitalize those that are recoverable, many of these valuable properties may be lost to liberal churches, Muslim mosques, land developers or condominium developers. God's people sacrificed for these church facilities and this is a great way to assure that they have a future filled with vitality and impact for the Gospel.

The High Impact
Church Revitalization Model

Few churches are able to do a high impact
church revitalization model. Those who are almost
always are supported by a mega church that decides to
give support to a once thriving church. For instance,
Pastor Johnny Hunt of Woodstock, Georgia has chosen
to utilize the high impact church revitalization model
with a church in Panama City, Florida. The Georgia
mega church and its leaders have poured large
amounts of resources, both physical as well as financial,
into the effort and it is turning a declining church
around through the effort. Most churches needing to be
revitalized do not have such a generous church and I
thank the Lord for this effort by a key influential pastor

and his people. Usually it takes a large regional church or several churches to rebirth these works as self-sustaining, self-supporting, and full service congregations.

Organizational Learning Church Revitalization Model

Churches that decide to work towards revitalization and renewal through a personal desire of individual members and lay leaders are referred to as an organizational learning revitalization model. This is when church members take it upon themselves to learn the principles and practices for bringing about church renewal. This model works best with a church that has little or no entrenchment and is an easy candidate to consider church renewal. When a plateaued church can learn from a written work and a few skill sets that will allow it to refocus its ministry, there are relatively few

obstacles hindering this process and it has a great

chance of repairing those things which are keeping the

church from demonstrating growth.

Program Driven
Church Revitalization Model

Most church organizations invest significant

amounts of time, energy and money into creating

programs and events for people they hope to serve. I

am inspired by the countless hours of work that many

of these organizations put into these important projects.

These churches are a better place because of their work.

Many a church finds themselves locked into a series of

programs which sufficed in the past and are unable to

resist the urge to retain what had worked previously,

though it is no longer helping the church and its

ministry to impact their community. We live in a rapidly changing world, and it is safe to say you cannot assume that what has worked in the past will work today or in the future. We must all continue to evaluate our efforts based on the feedback and input we receive from the very church members and potential prospects we serve.

Designing a workable church revitalization strategy utilizing the program-driven church revitalization model must take into account the possibility that if we are not careful, we may end up creating programs and events for people who no longer exist within our communities other than inside the memory of our past successes. This model will minister to people and grow through a variety of church programs. These programs will consist of some combination of evangelism, discipleship, youth, children, men, women ministries, music, missions, and social ministries. This church model is driven by program. In other words, its major organizing principle is program or a mix of programs. Its strategy to accomplish its mission is by nature program. Its primary value is program. The non-negotiable in the church renewal effort is that it will revolve around certain programs. The building blocks of the church revitalization project are programs. If the usual response to new ideas in your church is, *"We've never done it that way before,"* chances are you have a program-based church revitalization model.

Program-driven revitalization models tend to be staff, dollar and worker intensive. While offering quality programs that seek to reach a community, they require much expertise and energy. Churches that succeed in providing quality programming are usually rewarded with growth, recognition and prosperity. Those which do not meet the quality quotient, are lost in irrelevance. Program-driven church revitalization tends to be clergy-led, building-centered and institutional in nature. The older generation tends to prefer program-based churches because they best express the institutional and stability values of builders. Suburbia and county seat churches have had great success with the program-based renewal approach. Some have accused program-based churches of fostering a consumer Christian mentality. If you choose to utilize this model for church revitalization by offering new programs that will replace some of your existing ones, remember to keep refining your programs and what you do and how you do it. The real people we serve and will eventually serve will thank you for it.

Portable Church Based
Church Revitalization Model

Those using this model for church revitalization and renewal usually fall into two basic groups. The first group to use this model is a church that gets in trouble with building expansion and is unable to continue to support the indebtedness of their property, so they sell it off to another church by allowing it to take over the declining church's debt and begin a new campus. When that happens sometimes the membership will stay, but there are other times where the former church moves to a portable church meeting in something less expensive while they regroup.

The second group that often uses this model are those who need a temporary means to move its membership out of the present facilities so the physical plant might be renovated and remodeled. Churches of all sizes have done this model as a means to go portable for a season so either a new building could be built or a present facility be remodeled and refurbished. Two of my churches where I serve in central Florida have done this. One moved to a nearby school for eighteen months while the sanctuary was built and the other put up a SPRUNG Structure[30] building on their property so they could continue to utilize the rest of their facilities while the sanctuary was totally reconstructed.

[30] If you would like further information regarding SPRUNG Structure buildings go to: http://www.sprung.com .

When you are forced to consider a portable church model it would be wise to consider the duration and need before you jump into a long-term facility once again.

The Multi-Site Church Revitalization Model

The idea of going multi-site for the purpose of church revitalization is a model which many healthy churches are considering as a means to assist churches that are in decline. Not all of the multi-site churches are going multisite for the purpose of revitalization, yet there are those which see it as a means to strengthen a declining church through the brand strength of a healthy growing church.

Launching into any conversation about the possibility of going multi-site begins with a growing understanding of what multi-site is about and discovering how it can help your church better fulfill the Great Commission! An estimated 1000 to 2000 churches nationwide are experimenting with this concept: one church (meaning one staff, one board, one budget) meeting in multiple locations, usually with the various sites developing unique personalities, yet sharing the same "brand identity" and DNA. There are an estimated 3,000 multisite churches in the United States. Many involved in the multi-site model for revitalization have experienced God's hand upon their individual ministries and have seen more people than ever expected come to faith in Christ. These churches are driven by a passion for church revitalization and renewal as a means to see more people come to Christ.

When utilized as a revitalization model there is a clear vision and an understanding of their specific purpose for renewal in their communities. Church revitalization pastors from all church sizes have come to the conclusion that the multi-site church revitalization model is the tool they need to fulfill the call of God upon their churches and those they are seeking to restore.

Here are some interesting facts about the rise of the multi-site model:

☐ Multi-sites now outnumber mega churches[31]

☐ Multi-site is mainstreaming and crossing cultures

☐ Multi-site is birthing other sites and churches

☐ Multi-sites reach more people and mobilize more volunteers

---

[31] Bird, Warren and Kristin Walters. Multisite is Multiplying (Dallas, TX: Leadership Network, 2010), 2.

☐ Multi-sites have a 90% success rate

☐ In 2007, 16% of protestant pastors indicated that their churches were seriously exploring the multi-site renovation model.

At the heart of an effective multi-site model, you will find four core beliefs or forces driving the strategy. The first is a passion to see the Great Commission fulfilled. Second, in most cases it begins with a vision to reach a city with the gospel. It allows a church the opportunity to reverse its approach to ministry – instead of expecting people to come to one central location, the church goes to the people, it moves into their community – on to their turf. Third, it is driven by the belief that the DNA or health of the original church is worthy of reproduction or transference into churches in need of revitalization as an effort to reach further into communities.

Multi-site is not exclusively a mega church phenomenon. Multi-site churches can be found across the entire size spectrum, with the average size range of churches who are doing multi-site worship getting smaller. The median size for a multi-site church is 1,300 including all of its campuses, with 1 in 4 having a total worship attendance at all campuses being less than 1,000.[32] Over 3,000 churches are utilizing multi-site.[33] Research suggests that among the ten fastest growing churches in the United States, 70 percent use multiple venues or multiple campuses.[34] Other research indicates that among the ten largest churches in the United States, 90 percent use multiple venues or multiple campuses.[35] Two thirds of multi-site churches are connected to a denomination.[36] The majority of multi-sites (85%) have 3 or fewer geographic campuses

[32] Bird, Warren and Kristin Walters. Multisite is Multiplying (Dallas, TX: Leadership Network, 2010), 11.

[33] Surratt, Geoff, Greg Ligon and Warren Bird. *The Multi-Site Church Revolution* (Grand Rapids, MI: Zondervan, 2006), 2.

[34] Ibid., 21.

[35] Ibid., 21.

[36] Bird, Warren and Kristin Walters. Multisite is Multiplying (Dallas, TX: Leadership Network, 2010), 2.

– and 7 services total.[37] One in three multi-sites added a campus through a merger.[38]

While utilizing the multisite church revitalization model, these churches are embracing other churches and their facilities all across America. It has been predicted that there will be twenty to thirty thousand more multisite locations set up in existing church buildings over the next decade. This model is a great way for a hurting and declining church to be re-strengthened by giving it the impetus of people, finances, and new vision it needs for revitalization.

Church Merger Church Revitalization Model

The idea of the church merger revitalization model can be daunting. And because most mergers

---

[37] Bird, Warren and Kristin Walters. Multisite is Multiplying (Dallas, TX: Leadership Network, 2010), 4.

[38] Ibid., 9.

occur when one church is in financial difficulty, it's easy to feel, inaccurately so, that merging is an act of failure. According to Leadership Network research, two percent of United States Protestant churches have been part of a merger in the last two years. Another eight percent say they will probably merge in the next two years. Those two groups represent thirty thousand churches. Utilization of the church merger revitalization model can be, and often is, a creative means to achieving God's plan to reach one's community for Christ. Merging independent churches into a single church is a complex venture that does not always increase financial stability, enhance community benefit, or bring about God's hand on a ministry.

Before jumping into a merger, each congregation needs to take a "hard look" at who they are and what vision(s) they have for themselves as a church. The congregations also need to assess their motivation, readiness, willingness and suitability for a church merger. All alternatives to merging should be explored. The churches considering the Church Merger Revitalization model need to find out if they will be compatible. Each congregation has its own unique "congregational culture" and that includes, but is not limited to areas of worship, theology, leadership, views on women's roles in the church, use of space and time.

It is important to involve your staff early in the process. I have listed some questions that will help you get started in your Church Merger Revitalization model discernment progression:

Who are we today?

What is our history as a church?

What dreams and visions do we have for the future?

What are our strengths and weaknesses?

What is our financial situation? What assets do we have?

What is our current attendance at worship? At other church related events?

Have we experienced growth or decline over the past ten years?

What has this growth or decline been attributed to?

Does our church reflect the composition of the surrounding community?

Why do we want to consider a merger?

Are we dissatisfied with the status quo?
Can our mission goals be accomplished more successfully with another church than all alone?

Can we reach new people who do not necessarily reflect our current composition?

Are we interested in outreach and potential growth?

What characteristics do we have that would contribute to a successful merger?

Are we willing to take risks and be open to change?

Can we share power, leadership and decision-making?

Are we spiritually and financially healthy?

Can we be patient, flexible, and willing to compromise?

Are we willing to form new relationships?

Do we have enough time and energy to devote to the merger?

Do we have a commitment to grow both spiritually and numerically?

Are the pastors engaged and supportive of the church merger revitalization model?

Are they willing to work as colleagues?

Are we willing to accept the "other pastor" or a pastor not known to either congregation after our church merger?

Are we willing to accept any "fallout" from the merger?

Are we open to learning and working together with people who are racially and culturally different than we are?

Are we open to identifying and working on common mission goals with the other church?

Do we have a willingness to reach people in the community who do not necessarily reflect the current composition of the church?

The church merger revitalization model transpires when two or more churches decide to combine into one entity. Mergers and consolidations are technically different. If a merger creates a new entity, it is generally considered a consolidation. When one church absorbs one or more other churches, it is a merger. The idea of a merger usually doesn't just arrive in the church; something brings the idea to the table. Since merging is such a daunting prospect, and because a merger is often seen as a last resort, most churches considering church revitalization through this model undergo some serious thinking before contemplating a merger. The decision to undertake such a large degree of change can be precipitated by a variety of factors:

- A financial crisis or the belief that a crisis is nearing.
- The departure of a pastor or a patriarch.
- A proactive move to head off risk(s).
- A struggle to recruit or retain staff or talent.
- The suggestion of a creditor interested in preserving the church.
- A growth strategy arising from a strategic plan.
- A request to merge from another organization.

While the path that every merger takes is unique, there are six typical steps: an initiation phase, negotiation of the merger, a merger agreement, legal action, renewal launch, and the beginning of integration of multiple congregations. In real life, of course, these stages overlap and may fall in a different order. A new identity and the best chance for church renewal is the goal. Two or three small churches clattering under one roof like friendly roommates is not the ultimate goal. It is not always possible or practical to have a new property and building, but you can give the church a new name and declare it a new day and beginning of a new ministry.

Affinity Based Church Revitalization Model

When a community changes culturally around the declining church, consideration of launching the affinity-based church revitalization model could be considered. Since the former, once viable church is declining, it might represent a shift in a community towards a new people group coming into prominence. When this happens, utilizing this church revitalization model is a great way to still have influence and impact culture in the same geographical location. The culture can be defined ethnically, by language, socioeconomic factors, lifestyle preferences, or other distinguishing characteristics. The existing declining churches of North America will not be transformed to health and vitality by re-establishing more of the same churches we have now. They will be transformed by using the affinity-based church revitalization model to reach all types of groups. Here are some of the groups that need

to be considered if you select this model:

> Hispanic
> African American
> Korean
> Cambodian
> Russian
> Laotian
> Native American
> Vietnamese
> Filipino
> Haitian

There are other groups which might be considered, but

these are a great place to begin when praying about

utilizing this model for church renewal.

Mother to Daughter Based Church Revitalization Model

This model works when often a very traditional church seeks to connect with either less traditional communities or a younger population base than what presently attends the church's primary worship times. This takes on several forms, but often it either meets in another place on campus or off campus during non-worship times of the mother church. By launching the new mother to daughter model, it allows the present form of worship to go on uncorrupted and a new daughter model to begin targeted at a different community demographic. This is where the mother church assumes responsibilities of starting the daughter church in an effort to revitalize the former church without destroying a solid structure already in place and working fairly well. While many a church plant has been launched this way by "hiving off" of the mother church services, this model in church revitalization is different in that it does not seek to move others out of the traditional service, but launch an entirely new one reaching those who are not already connected with the primary services. Here are some of the strengths of considering this model:

Used often in healthy churches

Takes away a spirit of competition for existing members

Allows for time to build a core group

Daughter church develops a new independent leadership team

The risk is only in those seeking to build new group

Mother church offers resources necessary for the effort

One difficult challenge is knowing when and how the daughter church should cut the apron strings and become its own viable entity, yet remaining part of the initial church's outreach efforts. Mid-size to larger churches are better able to utilize this mother to daughter based church revitalization model. Very few denominational entities will be able to assist with this model because national agencies and state agencies are not able to provide a long-term effort. A local church network or an association is your best place to go for assistance in this model. They are the boots on the ground and can be of great help to the church working in this model.

Breaking Growth Obstacles Church Revitalization Model

Except for new church plants still in the infancy stage, churches tend to plateau at certain sizes. Almost everyone who has written on the subject has his or her version of the numerical growth obstacles, yet these basic obstacle levels are usually around:

> The thirty-five-growth obstacle
> The seventy-five-growth obstacle
> The one hundred twenty-five-growth obstacle
> The two hundred-growth obstacle
> The four hundred-growth obstacle
> The seven hundred-fifty-growth obstacle

There are hurdles that need to be considered in each of these numerical levels if a church desires to climb into the next level. Things that work in larger churches and offered by larger church pastors as forms for church revitalization almost always do not work for the smaller churches seeking to copy the effort.

Relocation
Church Revitalization Model

Sometimes even growing churches see the challenges of plateau or decline threatening if they choose to remain where they are currently located. When a thriving church is faced with a decline in its community, considering a move to another part of the community or a move to another totally different community is often a way to keep a church from getting stuck and facing eventual rapid decline. If this church revitalization model is to be considered, be sure to consider the cultural shifts and demographics of your target area. It must be a community that displays growth potential. A second challenge of this model will be discovering and securing a new meeting place that is more efficient for your revitalization effort. Often when utilizing this model, industrial buildings or larger warehouses are a great way to begin the church in the new area until you grow sufficiently in the new area and can make long term plans such as property acquisition and future facility expansion.

Having used this model of relocation myself, here are a few thoughts in reflection that might assist you in your decision.

- It is easier to relocate a younger church than an older one.
- Those members who are thirty years or older have difficulty making the move in many ways!
- You get smarter when you are in the middle of the relocation than you were at the beginning.

- Most church relocations are the result of a community's rapid expansion and the church is swallowed up.

- It is time to: either relocate, buy extra land or begin the process of rapidly downsizing the present ministry and face eventual decline.

- You will likely face intense conflict when considering any significant church revitalization process that points you toward relocation.

- Along your journey, your efforts in good planning will eventually encourage you. The other side of the coin is that your ignorance in the work of church relocation will likely and eventually humble you.

- Seek the advice of others often.

In the Book of Exodus, Moses asked Jethro over and over again for his counsel.[39] Begin early to cultivate a strong sense of Biblical urgency. Churches usually do not address problems until it is too late. By then they swamp the boat. Jesus' parables are a great place to start as an antidote to inertia. Preaching, teaching, organized prayer meetings for the specific purpose of relocation, special events, and personal testimonies can quicken a church's heartbeat to take the next step of faith. Sadly, complacency remains par for the course for most members during relocation projects. Avoiding such malady is critical. Identify and mobilize your key lay leaders. Enlist the support of your

---

[39] C.f. Exodus 18.

strong influencers. Get your early adopters and apostles moving the congregation forward. Do not use up your time placating and cajoling those who are fearful of the move. Keep your focus on the goal, and your hand on the throttle. Expect spiritual warfare. It is an indication that God is at work. Relocation pits the value of self-interest against the value of community outreach and expansion. Design a transition process to help members let go of what they know and love before asking them to embrace the uncertain future. Each setting demands a careful diagnostic assessment so that leaders can design a practical and relevant process. It is always easier looking back than seeing the challenges as they confront us. Hindsight is always twenty-twenty.

Bi-vocational Church Revitalization Model

A growing model that is springing up all over the country is the bi-vocational church revitalization model. This rise in popularity is often due to the local church not making or noticing the shifts necessary for the church to change before it is forced to consider this model. Many churches look at this revitalization model as the next to the last thing they can try before they utilize the legacy model and give the property over to the local association or revitalization network. The clergy in North America continues to change and evolve. Churches that were once able to have multiple full time staff members on salary are now considering moving towards this model. The bi-vocational church revitalizer has been on my mind lately. As our economy braces for ups and downs, the use of this type of church revitalizer is happening all over North America. Not only are pastors from smaller or more rural congregations utilizing this model, but even the smaller declining urban church or urban fringe church is utilizing this model. Of course, many inner-city pastors and ethnic pastors have been carrying on bi-vocational ministries for many years, but now it appears bi-vocational church revitalization ministries are popping up in the middle-class communities as well. Pastors with seminary degrees are being thrust into the field of bi-vocational church revitalization, as the church is unable to climb out of its present state of decline. The story rings true for pastors all across the nation. Students who are just graduating from seminaries of almost every denomination are facing the need to consider this model. Most of these potential candidates have little experience and a church locked in a state of plateau might seek a pastor from a seminary with little training, but with optimism and zeal.

A "Bi-vocational Church Revitalizer" is a term becoming more relevant today. It is a term that has been around for some time in the field of church planting, yet today it is a practice utilized by many a declining church. Where I serve in Central Florida, even with a large urban population center, it is a practical model that we have considered and are using. The men who serve these churches are faced with high cost of living and this model is the most practical ideal for the minister and his family. With the decline in numbers and the loss of critical mass in the local church, it is becoming a way of life that many pastors have two or more vocations. It has been suggested that in some states around America, the bi-vocational ministers group is as large as fifty percent. In the Alpha

Baptist Association in Tennessee, twenty-two of the twenty-five churches are led by a bi-vocational pastor.

The bi-vocational church revitalization model is a great model to help a church get back on its feet. These are not churches that have been forgotten, but are active fellowships that have a strong biblical presence. Not every pastor is able to consider becoming a bi-vocational minister. Not every minister is wired to be able to serve in two capacities. These ministers have the same schedule as most full-time ministers. They preach and teach. Those in the hospital are visited. Yet, they still have a full-time job outside of the church. Many a ministers' wife has worked outside of the home in order for the church to have a full-time minister. Yet in the realm of church revitalization, instead of the negative connotation, which many bi-vocational ministers have, the church revitalizer sees this as the only path to truly turn around the church and is willing to do it. Some of the finest preachers I know are serving in bi-vocational churches that are being revitalized through their efforts. These church revitalizers serve there because God has positioned them there.

We live in a post-Christendom world. The church's impact on culture is not what it was in the past. This might just be an opportunity for our greatest day! The church has a chance to re-experience its identity as a missionary people.

Remember, we are and have always been strangers and aliens in this land. But in a post-Christendom world, the essential of the clergy is no longer presumed. This is why the bi-vocational church revitalization model makes such great sense. With churches in a rapid state of decline, it is getting harder and harder to keep resourcing a large number of full-time pastors for our smaller churches. I see that there are at least nine extraordinary benefits to going bi-vocational when seeking to revitalize a church in decline:

- Bi-vocational church revitalizers are in touch with non-Christians.

- Bi-vocational church revitalizers have plenty of time to listen to the hearts of non-Christians.

- Bi-vocational church revitalizers have the advantage of living in the "real" world.

- Bi-vocational church revitalizers are better able to understand those regular people that walk the streets of our community.

- Bi-vocational church revitalizers endure unstable income, lack of job security, and long working hours in both ministry and their second job.

- Bi-vocational church revitalizers, like any other Christian or non-Christian, know how it feels to be juggling family, work and church responsibilities.

- Bi-vocational church revitalizers are constantly living and working with people in the world and this gives them more opportunities to share their lives with others, both Christians and non-Christians alike.

- Bi-vocational church revitalizers can have the greatest opportunities for personal evangelism.

- Bi-vocational church revitalizers are able to recognize and embrace more easily the popular culture of a community since they are working in the area and culture.

Bi-vocational revitalizers are special kind of men who will do whatever is required to serve the Lord wherever He leads them. We need more church revitalizers who are eager and skilled to serve as a bi-vocational renewal leader. The declining church needs those who can make their living outside the church, if necessary, and have that calling from God to be all that he can be in the church while serving Him. Lay people are beginning to see the great value of a bi-vocational church revitalizer. It is becoming an accepted model for the church revitalization community. When you consider the extremely large number of churches in the western hemisphere that average less than one hundred people on Sunday, it is a logical conclusion to draw for the future that more than sixty percent of our churches will be led by the bi-vocational church revitalizer.

Questions for Determining Your Church's Readiness to Begin in Renewal

With these models uncovered, there are a few questions to be answered in order to determine your church's readiness to get involved in church revitalization and renewal. How do you know if your church is ready to participate in church revitalization? Start with asking yourself these questions. The more you and your church can answer these questions affirmatively, the more prepared you are to begin the church revitalization process.

1) Do you and your people have a burden for lost people and a willingness to see your church revitalized and become healthy? Has a leader surfaced for the revitalization cause?

2) Has your congregation shown a willingness to step out in faith and try new things?

3) Do you have a vision for your city and region?

4) Is your congregation spiritually mature and able to discern God's movement?

5) Has your congregation practiced a generous spirit?

6) Are you willing to risk?

7) Does your congregation have a genuine kingdom mindset?

8) Are you willing to invest resources (people & finances) towards renewing your church?

Wrapping It Up!

In closing, I would like to share with you a few of the most common mistakes churches make when beginning in church revitalization and renewal. An initial mistake is that church revitalization is not modeled. If the leaders of the church are not experiencing spiritual renewal, the chances of the church experiencing renewal is limited. Secondly, church revitalization is not taught to the entire congregation. Nothing becomes a priority unless it is spoken about and taught on a regular schedule. Third, church revitalization is not simple or clearly defined. Do not make the process too complicated, however, or nothing will happen because your turnaround team members will always be confused. Fourth, the serendipitous moments in church revitalization are not celebrated. Make a big deal out of little victories, which will lead to bigger and bigger victories. Great things do not usually happen overnight. Fifth, measure what is going on. Numbers, noises and nickels do matter so share the good things that are happening in these areas during your church's renewal journey. Finally, church revitalization is not seen. Keep it on the forefront and not hidden somewhere. Let new people coming to your church see what is going on in your church's effort towards renewal.

APPENDIX

Key Church Revitalization and Renewal Definitions

While the field of church revitalization and renewal is ever expanding, along with key terms relating to this field, here are some of the key fundamental definitions relating to this field of study:

Absence of the Serendipitous Moment: The more a church is under stress the less it feels God's presence! Do not hear me say that God abandons stuck churches, rather I believe the whirlwind, earthquake and conflagration of a church in turmoil makes it all the more difficult to perceive the still small voice of a Holy God. The greater the anxiety, conflict, and unyielding stagnation in a congregation, the less the church experiences those serendipitous, coincidental little miracles which seem to indicate the presence of the Holy Spirit alive and at work with one's church.

Adoption: When a stronger healthy church is willing to embrace a sick and declining church to help it get back on its feet and growing again. Usually a covenant takes place between the adopting church and the church being adopted through a covenant.

Affinity Churches: When churches use marketing preferences interests as an instrument to reach a specific target demographic these are referred to as affinity churches.

Annual Church Profile: The Annual Church Profile or ACP is a report that a local congregation completes each year and sends to its local Baptist association. In turn the local association passes the information along to the state convention, and eventually to the national convention. The Annual Church Profile (ACP) process exhibits the voluntary cooperation between local churches, associations, state conventions and the national entities.

Anxiety Shock Absorber: The leader who wants to bring about revitalization change in a congregation must become an anxiety shock absorber. A person with this quality can successfully resist the avalanche of anxiety that is bowling over everyone else within the fellowship. If you stay calm and demonstrate that you are not going to let the process of revitalization and renewal get derailed, it usually has a calming, quieting effect on the entire church.

Assimilation: Personal renewal precedes and leads to corporate revitalization. It's about changed people who courageously change structures. For deep change to come to an organization, its leaders must first go through a process of deep, personal change.

Bella Karoly Principle: In response to church revitalization changes, everybody loves you when you are mediocre but real change agents will be criticized for their hard work and commitment to renewal.

Biotic Capacity: The highest number of people a church can intuitively reach given its available assets.

Bi-Vocational Minister: When a minister does not serve the church on a full-time basis and has a full-time secular occupation.

Blocker: The Blocker is one who struggles with changes and methodologies. They will often work towards defeating something mainly because of not possessing the ability to handle change.

Breakthrough: Positive change occurs when we uncover the work of God and align ourselves to His purposes. Most people learn best through discovery. The ultimate discovery of God's vision is the key to facilitating deep and lasting change in the local congregation.

Catalytic Event: As a church deals with its stuckness, most often it will see in the reoccurring patterns that lead back to a catalytic event which served as a critical moment from which the germs of paralysis began to take hold of the church fellowship. The principle is that the negative patterns in a church's life began at an event or a small series of events, which radically and perpetually altered the life of the congregation.

Change Agent: One who seeks to make changes in accordance with a pre-developed strategic plan in an effort to revitalize and renew a dying church. These individuals work towards engaging others in a new norm of growth and advancement while managing people's resistance and anxieties.

Church Cul-de-sacs: This occurs when you turn to the left or the right and find your church in a continual circle moving but with no real advancement. These are the churches that are prime for restarts.

Church Cut-Off: A relationship that has been indefinitely, perhaps even permanently severed.

Church Deserters: These individuals are basically made up of three types of church attenders, which bring harm to any church revitalization effort. They are those who merely sit back and look over the church passing judgment on what is or is not happening. The first one is the lay looker, who are there for a time but are gone just about the time you get to know their name. Then they are followed by the lay leavers who are gone at the first hint that more is going to be expected from them than had been expected in the past. The last group of church deserters is the lay losers. Lay losers are the ones who want everything to be a lose/win for their point of view and opt out of the renewal effort as soon as their side cannot win.

Church Genograms: Diagrams of family trees that filter in and out of the congregation. These include those who are longtime members, active members, weekly attenders, and those who have a mere casual acquaintance with the church during special events.

Church Growth Movement: This term means different things to different people who use it. As used in this series, it refers to the movement that began in the 1960's primarily through the inspiration of Dr. Donald A. McGavran. It refers to a comprehensive way of understanding the growth and spread of the Christian movement. This movement brought missionary practices to the western hemisphere. Its fundamental tenet was that God intended the church to grow.

Church Revitalization Assistance Team: This team works to help the struggling church in decline to begin to develop tools necessary for the turnaround of a dying or plateaued church. It is usually made up of outside individuals from the church being assisted, as it takes much energy and synergy that declining churches usually have not maintained.

Church Revitalization Cluster Groups: Cluster groups offer pastors from multiple churches who are involved in the *Church Revitalization Coaching Network* to become part of this continuous learning cluster that includes other active church revitalizing pastors going through the network coaching to collaborate together. The renewal pastor can continue being a part of this cluster as long as the church continues to work on its recommendations or up to 36 months.

Church Revitalization Coaching Network: is a skilled renewal coach who works directly with individual pastors and churches who desire assistance as well as willing to go through a Church Renewal Journey and accept the recommendations provided by the Church Revitalization Network. This coach will provide a listening ear, ask pertinent questions, and expect accountability in fulfilling the recommendations. This process is a three-year journey and churches can become involved once a year beginning in May. The strength of this network for churches in need of revitalization is the weekly interaction with key practioners, monthly coach to the church peer learning group, and a practioner coach available daily if needed for guidance.

Church Revitalization Definition: A movement within in protestant evangelicalism which emphasizes the missional work of turning a plateau or declining church around and moving it back towards growth.

Church Revitalization Initiative: Is when a local church begins to work on the renewal of the church with a concerted effort to see the ministry revitalized and the church become healthy.

Collaborative Leader: The leader who allows those he works with to assist in making decisions based on their involvement in the decision-making process.

Concentric Circles: Circles within circles are called concentric circles.

Conflict: is a problem to be solved that includes personalities and emotions that have lined up in opposition to each other. In fact, a conflicted situation usually contains multiple problems.

Conflict Avoidance: is the refusal to acknowledge and/or deal with conflict.

Conflict Crisis: is the eruption and outburst that happens in a crisis due to unresolved agendas.

Conflict Hibernation: is hidden below the surface, and is generally peaceful, but problems will resurface later with greater intensity if they are left unresolved.

Continuous Learning Community: are small groups of individuals who come together in a learning environment for an extended period of time led by trained facilitators. They focus on leadership teaching, accountability and peer mentoring.

Controlling Leadership: Church leadership who quits providing spiritual direction and begins to operate as organizational controllers.

Consumer Christians: Church hoppers who move from church to church to church seeking the latest feel good easy worship moment over the hard task of renewal.

Cosmology: Another word for worldview. It describes how people look at and seek to interpret the world around them.

Creative Programming: Constant creativity, the willingness of a church to dare something new in worship or to risk being led by a different person or different sort of person is an indication of real life in a congregation.

Custodians: are church leaders who have become masters of inactivity within the local church. They fear changes, fail to adapt to changing environments, and eventually lead the church into death.

De-Churched: The expression given to people who have had damaging incidents within a local church and are no longer active in church in general.

Declining Church: Is any church that at one point in time flourished, but now faces spiritual, physical, and numerical failure and is in danger of being dissolved.

Demographics: Demographics are simply characteristics about a population of people. They are used in market research and by governments. Commonly examined demographics include gender, race, age, disabilities, mobility, home ownership, employment status, and even location. Demographic trends describe the historical changes in demographics in a population over time (for example, the average age of a population may increase or decrease over time). Both distributions and trends of values within a demographic variable are of interest. Demographics are about the population of a region and the culture of the people there.

Dictatorial Leader: A leader which functions as a commander and operates from a tyrannical position.

Dropout rate: New and longtime church members are leaving for other churches in the community, or they are leaving the local church completely.

E-0 Evangelism: Used to describe outreach among nominal church members. There is no increase in church membership when they come to Christ because their names are already on church rolls.

E-1 Evangelism: Used to describe outreach among non-believers who are in the same cultural group as those doing the evangelizing.

E-2 Evangelism: Used to describe outreach among non-believers who are culturally "near neighbors". They may speak a related language though it might not be mutually understood. An example would be German, French, English and Spanish people who have a similar cultural background even though they may not be able to understand one another's language.

E-3 Evangelism: Used to describe outreach among non-believers who are very different from our own cultural group. Their language, customs and worldview are completely foreign to us. These are our culturally distant neighbors.

Emperor's New Clothes Phenomenon: The inability to see in our subconscious the obvious realities all around us.

Entrance Points: are those unique opportunities for connection that a local church has which will draw prospects into the church. Most stuck churches need to add a minimum of eight new entrance points into the church to begin a movement towards turnaround.

Ethnicity: The characteristics of a given ethnic or people group.

Evangelization: For our purposes within church revitalization, evangelization takes place when the Gospel has been presented in such a way that those hearing it are capable of making an intelligent decision - yes or no - regarding Jesus as Lord and Savior.

Fault Lines of Renewal: Renewal fault lines are the merging points, the weakest links, which give way in a local church when the underlying forces become too much to handle. As opposing sides cease to coexist with one another, they will begin tearing the church apart. The distracting symptoms, which are not the real issue, are really only the fault lines in the church renewal struggle. They are not the underlying problems, but symptoms which emerged in the midst of revitalization.

Fringe Participants: As a failing marriage between the church and the pastor begins, often a leader in trouble will begin to place huge emphasis on the fringe participants in hope to revitalize his leadership status within a church. Remember we do not call them fringe participants for nothing. Fringe participants are less active, committed, and supportive of the real needs of the church.

Gatekeepers: some hold church power by keeping things from happening, preventing or allowing issues to be aired or addressed. Tenure is often a way a gatekeeper exercises control.

GOAL Pastoral Leadership Development: The Greater Orlando Adventures in Leadership pastoral leadership development is a voluntary, two-year, small group, peer learning experience for pastors that involves trained coaching, in-depth reading and mutual encouragement. It provides pastors with various tools for training laity and helps them develop strategies and skill sets for congregational transformation. It further develops the leadership competencies of pastors to enable them to better lead themselves and their church.

Ground Zero: In order to get to where you want to go you must know first where you have come from. You need to discover the church's ground zero! Once you have discovered and understand the church's past, you will be better able to move it forward into a better future. It is imperative that you take a realistic look at where your church stands in relation to health, present challenges as well as opportunities! Understanding your "Ground Zero" is the beginning of the journey and not the end.

Health: Healthy churches produce more and better disciples. Church health is about creating an ongoing culture of renewal and life. A healthy church will be a growing church naturally.

Historical Drift: The term utilized to describe the predisposition for organizations to depart over time from their foundational beliefs and practices.

Historical Knowledge: Stuck churches have a history of how they got stuck and often only those who have historical knowledge will be able to communicate to a church revitalizer the possible ways the church became polarized and stuck.

Homogeneous Unit: Used to define a group of people having a collective set of characteristics. They may speak the same language, participate in the same profession or have a similar cultural background.

Influencer: is anyone who is able to exercise significant influence over the people, the focus or the future of a church, ministry, or organization. Influencers can alter congregational conduct by supporting or boycotting ministries, withholding resources, or using their influence to influence votes.

Intentional Catalyst: Some leaders enter the revitalization process out of need to revitalize a church that had in former days been quite effective, but through various circumstances has become anemic due to cultural shifts and community transition in the primary ministry area. These leaders usually must work to stabilize the effort and then begin a slow process of bringing health to the work and ministry.

Inwardly Focused: The inwardly focused church has few outwardly focused ministries. Budget dollars in the church are spent on the desires and comforts of its church members. The staff spends most of its time taking care of members, doing maintenance ministry, with little time to reach out and minister to the community the church is supposed to serve.

Leader Dependent: When a church is dependent upon one single leader due to the failure to train and equip the laity for ministry the church becomes leader dependent instead of people centered.

Leadership: Everything rises and falls on leadership. Leaders must step forward and catalyze people to a greater passion for God and His purposes. The church can only be changed if its leadership is strengthened and functions effectively through empowerment.

Macro-Community: is the self-governing small township with a populace of 25,000 or less that is capable of delivering its residents with all of their essential needs and services.

Macro-Revitalization: An attempt at church revitalization, characterized by supplying programmatic information to the church and its leadership or offering training, but to those who are not immediately or directly involved with them.

Mega-Community: is an urban center with a populace of more than 25,000 where large numbers of individuals congregate within its borders.

Mega-Church: is the church that is located within a mega-community with a massive population at its fingertips. It is a body of believers with many thousands within a few-mile grid.

Micro-Church: is the local church that is located within the macro-community that is able to deliver to its congregants all of their spiritual and related needs from one singular church body.

Micro-Revitalization: An attempt at church revitalization, which is personally involved with the local church and its key leadership in an ongoing affiliation of sponsorship, partnership, supervision, mentoring, and coaching.

Maintainer: The maintainer desires the enhancement of the current state.

Manipulative Leader: A leader functions as a controlling force and seeks to hard sell his followers into what he desires. Ministry by coercion is the fashion of this type of leader.

Manipulators: are church leaders who are quite active in the local church as they place their own personal needs above the needs of the congregation. Members under this form of leadership become merely tools in a game played by those who seek personal reward.

Matriarchs: Like the patriarchs in a church, these are long term leaders who have been in a local church and have gained a degree of leadership priority through tenure. These individuals are not as strong as the patriarchs but have been given similar influence by the patriarchs due to similar beliefs and willingness to align with the former group.

Mergers: Is when a healthy church seeks to merge another unhealthy church into full membership. This is where the two shall become one. Rarely does it actually happen this way. Mergers are friendly take overs for the best of the Kingdom and both parties. Remember that 50 plus 50 does not equal 100! It usually equals 65.

Missional Church: is designed to connect with the different cultures around them and reach out into their target community. They take the church out of the red brick building and into the community. The opposite type of church is the Receptor Church which is designed to hold those who find the church rather than those who the church discovers.

Momentum Takers: This is the type of leader who is more in it for themselves than they are in it for those they serve.

Never-Churched: The term attached to individuals who have never been involved in the life of the church.

Nostalgia Churches: Are dying churches living in the past where the emphasis is on tradition rather than advancement. A hopeful return backwards to the church's glory days is what is desired, yet once they get there they find it is unrewarding and all consuming. Nostalgia churches are often more focused on the past and living in past glories then they are present realities. While it is important to honor the past in order to move successfully into the future it is just as important not to live in it! Nostalgia can lead to destruction.

Nudge List: Churches that are falling back into becoming legacy churches often need the nudge to get going again. Think about ideas and ways (nudges) that will send a simple message to the community that you are doing a new thing.

Old Blood Congregations: Churches that are adult-heavy are often prone to ministry failure. Old blood churches tend to focus everything inward, committing all their resources to internal service or maintenance, and slowly become anonymous in their community.

Opinion setters: those who hold the power because of visible influence in decision making.

Outreach/Maintenance Compendium: is when equilibrium between reaching the lost of one's community through outreach and the building up of those who are already saved and part of the local church (maintenance), the congregation will decline.

Paradigm Shift: Pronounced "Para-dime". A paradigm is a framework into which we fit ideas that we hold to be valid. It provides order for arranging how we look at the world. When one changes the primary way he or she looks at the world, we call that "paradigm shift". The most profound paradigm shift for the Christian is the conversion experience.

Pastor Chaplain: The rank and file church member views the pastor as their personal chaplain, expecting him to be on call twenty-four hours a day for their needs and preferences. When he fails to meet their expectations criticism usually follows.

Patriarchs: are long term church members which lead the church through influence which has been gained from tenure. These are often the most resistant to any change within a local church.

Plateaued Church: is a church that is neither growing nor declining but is in a perpetual state of polarization and unable to move forward to seek health. Such churches have a rate of growth roughly equivalent to the rate of attrition.

Polarization: Creates an organizational climate in which members mistake one another for the enemy and fall into conflict.

Polarized Congregations: Polarity literally means to draw individuals to one pole or another. Therefore, a polarized congregation is one in which it is the tendency of church folks to choose sides. In a polarized church, there are extreme cliques to the point that certain groups of people invariably tend to side together on every issue, tend to distrust other groups, and tend to view themselves as the only steadfast keepers of the flame of truth! Polarized congregations are church splits looking for a reason to happen!

Producers: a successful leader of church revitalization in a local church is called a producer. It is their desire to make things better within the local church. They produce lasting results that enable the church to make the turn towards growth and health.

Rebirth: in the midst of decline and despair when the beginning signs of hope and promise surface a rebirthing is about to take place.

Receptor Churches: are churches designed to hold those who find the church rather than those who the church discovers? The opposite type of church is the Missional Church, which is designed to connect with the different cultures around them and reach out into their target community.

Reconciliation: The Bible says that Christ reconciled us to God (Romans 5:10; 2 Corinthians 5:18; Colossians 1:20-21). The fact that we needed reconciliation means that our relationship with God was broken. Since God is holy, we were the ones to blame. Our sin alienated us from Him. Romans 5:10 says that we were enemies of God: "For if, when we were God's enemies, we were reconciled to him through the death of his Son, how much more, having been reconciled, shall we be saved through his life!"

Refocusing: Refocusing is the third pillar and it helps churches that are growing but still need to set new challenges and look for new opportunities to expand their gospel witness into their target area. Questions such as: "What is your Biblical purpose?" and "Why do you exist as a congregation?" must be addressed. Looking at how God showed up in the past is a good way to get the church unstuck by addressing where it has been, how God has worked and anticipating what He holds for our future. Addressing the church's focus, vision and leading them to discover God's new direction is just the beginning of helping a congregation to begin refocusing towards the Lord's new calling plan for the church. Many a pastor today has never been taught how to grow a church and they feel quite stuck and in need of someone to come along side of them and challenge them to refocus themselves and the church.

Regeneration Pastor: is one who has the revitalization skill sets necessary for assisting a church in its turnaround efforts.

Reinvention: This sixth pillar of Church Revitalization deals with tools and techniques necessary to assist the church when it is necessary to reinvent itself to a changing community. When a church experiences a shift in the community makeup, often there will be to varying degrees, the need to redevelop a new experience for those who make up the new context! New experiences must replace old experiences. New practices likewise will replace old practices. A church that is experiencing the need for reinvention must take seriously the need and make the commitment for reinventing itself, revaluing itself, reforming itself, and reinvigorating itself to fit the new context.

Reinventors: The reinventors are those completely committed to the unceasing radical change necessary to bring about growth and renewal.

Renewal Prayer Team: For churches that choose to be a part of the Church Revitalization Coaching Network, this internal team will pray regularly for changes that help their congregation fulfill its vision for revitalization.

Repetitive Programming: is when a church is chained to the proverbial tether ball going around and around the same old ways without ever seeking new vitality. Once you have gone around and around in a circle long enough you just cannot move forward any longer.

Repotting: This is a kinder, more friendly term often used by those in the midst of restarting. It is the same strategy as restarting but some ministers feel they can handle this term better.

Reproduction: A revitalized church is one that is healthy enough to birth new life. Training leaders... parenting churches... helping other churches revitalize. This comes when we understand our place in God's big picture.

RENOVATE National Church Revitalization Conference: A national cross-denomination church revitalization conference, which meets annually in November to raise the thought and influence regarding various aspects of church revitalization and renewal. This group and its influencers are working towards creating a Church Revitalization Movement that will raise the level of revitalized churches within the Western hemisphere.

Restarting: The final Pillar of Church Revitalization is the hardest and often only happens once the church's patriarchs and matriarchs have tried everything else they could think of to grow the church with no success. When a sick church no longer has the courage to work through the various issues that led to its poor health, it is usually identified as being on life support and in need of a restart. This type of church has been flat-lined and is just holding on by means of its legacy and the faithful few who attend. Being aware of their "critical" condition, however, is not enough. They have to become convinced they need "major" surgical treatment. Changing the mindset of the residual membership can be very difficult. Most of these churches are peopled by senior adults. Change is often hard to come by. Until the church is ready to make drastic change, it is useless to become involved. There are thousands of churches like this all over America:

Some are Baptists, others are Methodists, even in the Assembly's you can find them, Presbyterians, the Lutherans have them, Congregational, Christian, and many others, waiting for a mission-minded congregation to get involved in offering "new life." One startling phenomena is there are churches today, that as the laity begin to depart this life often see nothing wrong with taking the church to the grave as well. That was never part of God's plan for the thing He gave up His life.

Restoration: This fifth area of Church Revitalization deals with things a church and a minister must go through when circumstances necessitate that a restoration process is required. Things such as: gaining a new and fresh understanding of the new prospect for the church, which is vital if success is in the church's future; inspiring new prospects with a vision that is both compelling and motivational; meeting new needs in order to give you a restored place among the community in which you seek to further minister; becoming prospect driven during these days of transition looking for new and yet to be reached opportunities to minister; crafting something that comes out of a community in flux and looking for ways to reconnect to the community where you once were firmly entrenched.

Restructuring: The term used to describe the changing of the church structure so that it becomes compatible with the culture in which it is located.

Re-visioning: Have you ever seen a church that once was alive and vital begin to lose its focus and drive for the cause of Christ? That is a church that needs to work on its re-visioning strategy. Any re-visioning strategy works to help churches dream new dreams and accomplish new goals that lead towards regrowing a healthy church. This strategy is designed for a weekend retreat tailored fit to foster a sense of ownership and team ship related to discovering a shared vision for the church. Understanding the critical milestones necessary for a new vision will help foster healthy church practices that might have been lost due to something as simple of achieving a great goal, and then God's children taking an ill-advised rest that resulted in a slowing of the momentum into a maintenance mentality.

Revitalization: A church in need of revitalization is described as one where: there is the plateauing or declining after a phase of initial expansion; the church experiences the beginning of a high turn-over of lay leaders; there becomes a shorter duration of stay of the fully assimilated people in the work; the church morale and momentum level drops; the church coasts for a brief time and then drops again, only to see the cycle of decline repeated again and again.

Revitalization Players: Those who are willing to count the cost towards church revitalization and seek to add to the church's efforts of renewal. These individuals are mission-conscious, servant-minded, able to deliver the goods, seek to help others succeed, able to make the tough calls or hard choices, and finish the course well.

Revitalization Pretenders: With the rise of the need for church revitalization in our churches today there are those who would rather act the part and look the part but fall short of fulfilling the part of putting in the effort needed for revitalization. These individuals are revitalization pretenders who masquerade as being concerned for renewal but are not willing to put in the time or pay the price for revitalizing the church.

Sending Culture: creating a sending philosophy is indispensable to revitalizing a church. Churches that are revitalized see themselves as communities on mission with God, not as country clubs for Christians.

Servant Leader: Is a leader who leads through service to others. These leaders exemplify Christ-likeness.

Silver Tsunami: This term refers to the impact of the baby boomer generation is making in retirement. These active seniors bring vitality and active lifestyles into churches that have the ability to cater to their needs. A passive style of retirement found in previous generations is not part of this generation.

Skunking: Skunking is the phenomenon that happens frequently within local church renewal efforts, when pessimistic church members spray negativity all over those creative church members who are trying to spark the renewal efforts of the church. A well-known example would be the tried but true expression by skunkers "We tried that years ago and it did not work."

Sovereignty: A new work of God requires our personal surrender as well as our structures. We must release control and embrace ambiguity. Revitalization is not a "cookie-cutter" or "program" approach. God's vision for every church is unique and special. Revitalization will look different in each setting.

Steeple Jacking: Is when once sizable churches face the pain of shrinking congregations and are vulnerable to congregations with younger participants who become members of the vulnerable church in an effort to overtake their properties. The ambitious healthy church attempts to acquire at little or no cost the buildings and property of the shrinking church. This term refers to a merger is not a joint effort but more of a hostile takeover.

Stuck Church: Is a hurting church that displays symptoms of becoming or being stagnant, often paralyzed, numerically declining, strategically dormant, living locked in the past, or dying; it is the opposite of a flourishing and vibrant growing church.

Synergy: Positive change happens best in the context of relationship. By working together in cohorts for learning and encouragement, progress in the revitalization journey is accelerated, which is mutually beneficial to everyone involved.

Three-self Standard: Used to describe indigenous churches which stand on their own two feet. Such churches are often described as being self-supporting, self-governing and self-propagating.

Triangling: is the act of bringing in or drawing in a third party to add stability to a relationship. Adding a third party will often stabilize a relationship, especially if it is an intense relationship.

Unfriendly Take Over: A new type of church merger is arising in the western hemisphere. It occurs when relatively healthy churches are desperate for partners to validate and credibly reach other cultures or alliances that can provide resources to expand the mission that are unobtainable from denominational or cross-sector sources. These churches usually will force a cultural church to align through some sort of hostile takeover. While there are many healthy churches that are part of friendly takeovers where there is a win-win, it is this last group that ought to be avoided at all costs. A new term defines these hostile takeovers as steeple jacking.

Yesterday's Commentators: One of the biggest challenges to change towards revitalization is the number of yesterday's commentators a church possesses. These are the tribe that simply just kills any momentum gained toward renewal through a backwards view that seeks to anchor them in the past unable to make any steps toward the future.

Suggested Church Revitalization and Renewal Bibliography

Anderson, Leith. *A Church for the 21st Century: Bringing Change to Your Church to Meet the Challenges of a Changing Society.* Minneapolis: Bethany House Publishers, 1992.

_____. *Dying for Change: An Arresting Look at the New Realities Confronting Churches and Para-Church Ministries.* Minneapolis: Bethany House Publishers, 1998.

Anyabwile, Thabiti M. *What Is a Healthy Church Member?* Wheaton, IL: Crossway Books, 2008.

Arn, Win. *The Church Growth Ratio Book: How to Have a Revitalized, Healthy Growing, Loving Church.* Pasadena, CA: Church Growth, Inc., 1987.

Avery, William O. *Revitalizing Congregations: Refocusing and Healing through Transitions.* Herndon, VA: Alban Institute, 2002.

Baker, R. D., Truman Brown, Jr., and Robert D. Dale. *Reviving the Plateaued Church.* Nashville: Convention Press, 1991.

Barna, George. *Grow Your Church from the Outside.* Ventura, CA: Regal Books, 2002.

_____. *Turn-Around Churches: How to Overcome Barriers to Growth and Bring New Life to an Established Church.* Ventura, CA: Regal Books. 1993.

Batson, Howard K. *Common-sense Church Growth.* Macon: Smyth & Helwys, 1999.

Becker, Paul. *Seeing Your Vision Come True.* Oceanside, CA: Dynamic Church Planting International, 2007.

Benedict, Melanie. "From Embers to a Flame: Revitalizing Churches" *byFaith: The Web Magazine of the Presbyterian Church in America*

http://byfaithonline.com/page/in-the-church/from-embers-to-a-flame-revitalizing-churches (accessed October 10, 2010).

Berkley, James D. "Burning Out, Rusting Out, or Holding Out?" *Leadership a Practical Journal for Church Leaders* Volume IV (Winter 1983): 36-40.

Bickers, Dennis. "Bivocational Ministry: Meeting the Leadership Needs of the Smaller Church" *Rev: Revving Up Ministry Together*, November/December, 2008.

Bierly, Steve R. *Help for the Small Church Pastor: Unlocking the Potential of Your Congregation.* Grand Rapids: Zondervan, 1995.

_____. *How to Thrive as a Small-Church Pastor: A Guide to Spiritual and Emotional Well-Being.* Grand Rapids: Zondervan, 1998.

Bird, Warren and Kristin Walters. *Multisite is Multiplying,* Dallas, TX: Leadership Network, 2010, 2.

Blackaby, Henry. *Holiness: God's Plan for Fullness of Life.* Nashville: Thomas Nelson Publishers, 2003.

Blackaby, Henry T., Henry Brandt, and Kerry L. Skinner. *The Power of the Call.* Nashville: Broadman & Holman Publishers, 1997.

Borden, Paul D. *Hit the Bullseye.* Abingdon Press, Nashville. 2003.

Boschman, LaMar. *Future Worship.* Renew Books, Ventura, CA. 1999.

Bossidy, Larry, and Charan, Ram. *Execution.* New York: Crown Business, 2002.

Bowden, Boyce. "Different Paths to a Common Goal: Healthy, Revitalized Churches Making Disciples" *Interpreter Magazine Online* http://www.interpretermagazine.org/interior.asp?ptid=43&mid=11764 (accessed October 10, 2010).

Brady, Tom. "Missional Mergers: 9 keys to Success." *Outreach*, May/June, 2009.

Brown, R. D., Truman Dale, and Robert D. Baker. *Reviving the Plateaued Church.* Nashville: Convention Press, 1991.

Brunson, Mac and Ergun Caner. *Why Churches Die: Diagnosing Lethal Poisons in the Body of Christ.* Nashville: B&H Publishing Group, 2005.

Bubna, Don. "Ten Reasons Not to Resign," *Leadership a Practical Journal for Church Leaders* Volume XXVI (Fall 2005): 74-80.

Bubna, Donald, Keith Walker and Jim VanYperen. "20 Questions to Determine Your Church's Health," *Leadership a Practical Journal for Church Leaders* Volume XVIII (Spring 1997): 41-42.

Bunker, Kerry A. and Michael Wakefield. *Leading with Authenticity in Times of Transition.* Greensboro, NC: Center for Creative Leadership Press, 2005.

Buttry, Daniel. *Bring Your Church Back to Life: Beyond Survival Mentality.* Valley Forge: Judson Press, 1988.

Callahan, Kennon L. *Effective Church Leadership: Building on the Twelve Keys*. San Francisco: Jossey-Bass, 1990.

_____. *Small, Strong Congregations: Creating Strengths and Health for Your Congregation*. San Francisco: Jossey-Bass, 2000.

Cameron, Kirt and Ray Comfort. *The School of Biblical Evangelism: 101 Lessons*. Alachua, FL: Bridge-Logos, 2004.

Cha, Peter S., Steve Kang, and Helen Lee. ed. *Growing Healthy Asian American Churches: Ministry Insights from Groundbreaking Congregations*. Downers Grove, IL: Inter Varsity Press, 2006.

Chadwick, William. *Stealing Sheep: The Church's Hidden Problem with Transfer Growth*. Downers Grove, IL: Inter Varsity Press, 2001.

Cheyney, Tom. *Lessons Learned the Hard Way in Church Revitalization and Renewal* Orlando: Renovate Publishing group available from RenovateConference.org/bookstore.

Cheyney, Tom, David Putman, and Van Sanders. gen. eds. *Seven Steps for Planting Churches: Planter Edition*. Alpharetta, GA: North American Mission Board, 2003.

Christy, Mark. *Breaking Numerical Barriers and Revitalizing Plateaued Churches*. Amazon Digital Services Inc., 2012.

Clarensau, Michael H., Sylvia, Lee, and Steven R. Mills. *We Build People: Making Disciples for the 21st Century.* Springfield: Gospel Publishing House, 1998.

Clegg, Tom. *Missing in America: Making an Eternal Difference in the World Next Door.* Group, Loveland, Colorado. 2007.

Cole, Neil. *Organic Leadership: Leading Naturally Right Where You Are.* Grand Rapids: Baker Books, 2009.

Collins, James. *Good to Great.* Harper Business Essentials.

Conn, Harvey M. "Samples: Linking Strategy to Model," in *Planting and Growing Urban Churches: from Dream to Reality*, ed. Harvie M. Conn (Grand Rapids, MI: Baker, 1997), 195.

Conner, Mark. *Transforming Your Church: Seven Strategic Shifts to Help You Successfully Navigate the 21st Century.* Tonbridge, Kent (England): Sovereign World, Ltd., 2000.

Coppedge, Anthony D. *The Reason Your Church Must Twitter: Making Your Ministry Contagious. E-book 2008.* http://twitterforchurches.com (accessed 10/26/2010).

Cordeiro, Wayne. *Doing Church as a Team: The Miracle of Teamwork and How It Transforms Churches.* Ventura: Regal Books, 2001.

Cordeiro, Wayne. *Leading on Empty: Refilling Your Tank and Renewing Your Passion*. Minneapolis: Bethany House Publishers, 2010.

Crandall, Ron. *Turnaround and Beyond: A Hopeful Future for Small Membership Churches*. Nashville: Abingdon Press, 2008. (rev. ed. of Turnaround Strategies for the Small Church. c 1995).

_____. *Turn Around Strategies for the Small Church.* Nashville: Abingdon Press, 1995.

Creps, Earl G., *Off-road Disciplines: Spiritual Adventures of Missional Leaders*. 1st ed. San Francisco: Jossey-Bass, 2006.

_____. *Reverse Mentoring: How Young Leaders Can Transform the Church and Why We Should Let Them*. San Francisco: Jossey-Bass, 2008.

Crow, Charles D. & Crow, Kenneth E. "The Church Growth Movement and the American Dream," *Grow Magazine*. Bethany, OK: Church of the Nazarene, 2003.
Download at: http://www.nazarene.org

Dale, Robert D. *Leadership for a Changing Church: Charting the Shape of the River*. Nashville: Abingdon Press, 1998.

_____. *To Dream Again: How to Help Your Church Come Alive*. Nashville: Broadman Press, 1983.

Davis, Ronald L. *The Revitalization of The African-American Baptist Church, Association and Convention: Addressing Organizational Structures, Pastoral Leadership, Racial Reconciliation, and Socio-Economic Issues.* Maitland, FL: Xulon Press, 2014.

Dever, Mark. *Nine Marks of a Healthy Church.* Wheaton: Crossway Books, 2000.

_____. *What is a Healthy Church?* Wheaton: Crossway Books, 2007.

Devine, Mark and Darrin Patrick. Replant: How a Dying Church Can Grow Again. David C. Cook, 2014.

DeYmaz, Mark. *Building a Healthy Multi-ethnic Church: Mandate, Commitments and Practices of a Diverse Congregation.* San Francisco: Jossey-Bass, 2007.

Dockery, David S., Ray Van Neste, and Jerry Tidwell, *Southern Baptists, Evangelicals and the Future of Denominationalism.* Nashville: B&H Publishing Group, 2011.

Dudley, Carl S. *Making the Small Church Effective.* Nashville: Abingdon Press, 1993.

Dudley, Carl S, and Sally A. Johnson. *Energizing the Congregation: Images That Shape Your Church's Ministry.* Louisville: Westminster John Knox Press, 1993.

Duin, Julia. *Quitting Church: Why the Faithful Are Fleeing and What to Do About It.* Grand Rapids: Baker Books, 2008.

Dunagin, Richard L., and Lyle E. Schaller. *Beyond These Walls: Building the Church in a Built-out Neighborhood.* Nashville: Abingdon Press. 1999.

Earman, Jeffrey M. *Resuscitating the Almost Dead: Breathing New Life into Your Church.* CreateSpace Independent Publishing, 2013.

Falwell, Jonathan. General ed. *Innovatechurch: Innovative Leadership for the Next Generation Church.* Nashville: B&H Publishing Group, 2008.

Faulkner, Brooks R. *Burnout in Ministry: How to Recognize It, How to Avoid It.* Nashville: Broadman Press, 1981.

Finke, Roger, and Rodney Stark. *The Churching of America 1776 – 2005: Winners and Losers in Our Religious Economy.* New Brunswick, New Jersey: Rutgers University Press, 2008.

Fletcher, Michael. *Overcoming Barriers to Growth: Proven Strategies for Taking Your Church to the Next Level.* Ada, MI: Bethany House, 2009.

Foster, Richard J. *Celebration of Discipline.* San Francisco: Harper Collins Publishers, 1998.

Foss, Michael F. Preaching for Revitalization. Christian Focus Publications, Ltd: Geanies House, Fearn, Ross-Shire, Scotland, 2006.

Fowler, Harry H. *Breaking Barriers of New Church Growth: Increasing Attendance from 0-150.* Rocky Mount, NC: Creative Growth Dynamics, Inc., 1988.

Frank, Dottie Escobedo. *Restart Your Church.* Nashville: Abingdon Press, 2012.

Frazee, Randy. *The Connecting Church: Beyond Small Groups to Authentic Community.* Grand Rapids, MI: Zondervan, 2001.

Friedman, Edwin H. *A Failure of Nerve: Leadership in the Age of the Quick Fix.* New York: Seabury Books, 2007.

George, Carl F. *Beyond 800: Transitioning for Greater Impact.* Diamond Bar, CA: MetaChurch Publishing, 1995.

_____. *Beyond 400: Transitioning for Greater Impact.* Diamond Bar, CA: MetaChurch Publishing, 1995.

George, Carl F. with C. Peter Wagner. *Beyond 200.* Diamond Bar, CA: MetaChurch Publishing, 1995.

_____. *How to Break Growth Barriers: Capturing Overlooked Opportunities for Church Growth.* Grand Rapids: Baker Book House, 1993.

Gerber, Michael. *E-Myth Revisited*. New York: Harper Collins Publishers, 1995.

Getz, Gene, and Joe Wall. *Effective Church Growth Strategies*. Nashville: Thomas Nelson Publishers, 2000.

Getz, Gene A. *The Measure of a Healthy Church*. Chicago: Moody Publishers, 2007.

Gibbs, Eddie. *ChurchNext: Quantum Changes in How We Do Ministry*. Downers Grove, IL: InterVarsity Press, 2000.

Gleason, Michael. *Building on Living Stones: New Testament Patterns and Principles of Renewal*. Grand Rapids: Kregel Academic Publications, 1996.

Godin, Seth. *The Dip: A Little Book that Teaches You When to Quit and When to Stick*. New York: Penguin Group, 2007.

Green, Matthew. "Megachurch Myths." *MinistryToday Magazine*. http://www.ministrytodaymag.com/index.php/features/12951-megachurch-myths May/June 2006, 46-47.

Green, Michael. *Thirty Years that Changed the World: The Book of Acts for Today*. Grand Rapids: William B. Eerdmans Publishing Company, 2002.

Groeschel, Craig. *It: How Churches and Leaders Can Get It and Keep It*. Grand Rapids: Zondervan, 2008.

"Growing Small and Medium Churches." *Journal of Evangelism and Missions*. Volume 9 (Spring 2010): Cordova, TN and Schenectady, NY: 2010.

Hadaway, C. Kirk. *Church Growth Principles*. Nashville: Broadman Press, 1991.

Halter, Hugh, and Matt Smay. *AND: The Gathered and Scattered Church*. Grand Rapids: Zondervan, 2010.

Hammett, Edward H. with James R. Pierce. *Reaching People Under 40 While Keeping People Over 60*. St. Louis, MO: Chalice Press, 2007.

Hammond, Thomas, and Steve Wilkes. "Church Conflict/Church Growth," *Journal of Evangelism and Missions* Volume Seven (Spring 2008): 3-11.

Harding, Kevass J. *Can These Bones Live: Bringing New Life to a Dying Church*? Nashville: Abingdon Press, 2007.

Harney, Kevin G. and Bob Bouwer. *The U-Turn Church: New Direction for Health and Growth*. Grand Rapids: Baker Books, 2011.

Harris, Joshua. *Stop Dating the Church: Fall in Love with the Family of God*. Colorado Springs: Multnomah Publishers, 2004.

Harrison, Rodney. *Seven Steps for Planting Churches: Partnering Churches Edition*. Alpharetta, GA: North American Mission Board, 2004.

Harrison, Rodney, Tom Cheyney, and Don Overstreet. *SPIN-OFF CHURCHES: How One Church Successfully Plants Another.* Nashville: B&H Publishing Group, 2008.

Hawkins, O.S. *Rebuilding: It's Never Too Late for a New Beginning.* Dallas: Annuity Board of the Southern Baptist Convention, 1999.

Hazelton, Paul N. *7 Steps to Revitalizing the Small-Town Church.* Kansas City: Beacon Hill Press, 1993.

Hemphill, Ken. *The Antioch Effect: 8 Characteristics of Highly Effective Churches.* Nashville: Broadman & Holman Publishers, 1994.

_____. *The Bonsai Theory of Church Growth.* Nashville: Broadman Press, 1991.

Hemphill, Ken and Mike James. *Velcro Church.* Nashville: Auxano Press, 2013.

Hendricks, William D. *Exit Interviews: Revealing Stories of Why People Are Leaving the Church.* Chicago: Moody Press, 1993.

Herrington, Jim, Mike Bonem, and James H. Furr. *Leading Congregational Change: A Practical Guide for the Transformational Journey.* San Francisco: Jossey-Bass, 2000.

Hirsch, Alan and Tim Catchim. *The Permanent Revolution: Apostolic Imagination and Practice for the 21st Century Church.* San Francisco: Jossey-Bass, 2012.

Holt, William R. *Effectiveness by the Numbers: Counting What Counts in the Church.* Nashville: Abingdon Press, 2007.

Hood, Pat. *The Sending Church: The Church Must Leave the Building.* Nashville: B&H Books, 2013.

House, Polly. "Small Churches Go Transformational" http://www.bpnews.net/bpnews.asp?Id=33765 (accessed September 28, 2010).

Howell Jr., Don N. *Servant of the Servant: A Biblical Theology of Leadership.* Eugene, OR: Wipf & Stock Publishers, 2003.

Hudnall, Todd. *Church, Come Forth: A Biblical Plan for Transformational Turnaround.* Nashville: CrossBooks, 2014.

Hull, Bill. *Seven Steps to Transform Your Church.* Grand Rapids: Fleming H. Revell, 1993.

_____. *The Disciple-Making Pastor: The Key to Building Healthy Christians in Today's Church.* Grand Rapids: Fleming H. Revell, 1988.

Hunt, Josh, *Change Your Church or Die.* CreateSpace Independent Publishing, 2014.

Irwin, L. Gail. *Toward the Better Country: Church Closure and Resurrection*. Resource Publications, 2014.

Iorg, Jeff. *The Painful Side of Leadership: Moving Forward Even When It Hurts.* Nashville: B&H Publishing Group. 2009.

Jackson, Anne. *Mad Church Disease: Overcoming the Burnout Epidemic*. Grand Rapids: Zondervan, 2009.

Johnson, Heather, and Lindy Lowry. "25 Ideas & Trends Reshaping the American Church," *Outreach*, January/February, 2009.

Jones, Peyton. *Church Zero: Raising 1st Century Churches out of the Ashes of the 21st Century Church*. David C. Cook, 2013.

Kaplan, Abraham. *The Conduct of Inquiry: Methodology for Behavioral Science* Louisville, KY: Chandler Publishing Company, 1964; reprint, London: Oxford, 1998, 268-272.

Keenan, Tracy. "Finding the Focal Point," *Leadership a Practical Journal for Church Leaders* Volume XVIII (Spring 1997): 35-36.

Keener, Ronald E. "Pulling Back from the Brink," *Church Executive*, November, 2008.

Kimball, Dan. *They Like Jesus But Not the Church: Insights from Emerging Generations.* Zondervan, Grand Rapids, MI. 2007.

Klassen, Ronald and John Koessler. *No Little Places: The Untapped Potential of the Small-Town Church.* Grand Rapids: Baker Books, 2002.

Kneisel, Harvey. *New Life for Declining Churches: New Hope, New Vision, New Strategy, New Life!* Houston: Macedonian Call Foundation, 1995.

Kotter, John P. *Leading Change.* Boston: Harvard Business School Press, 1996.

Lancaster, Lynne C. and David Stillman. *The M-factor: How the Millennial Generation is Rocking the Workplace.* New York: HarperCollins Publishers, 2010.

Laubach, David C. *12 Steps to Congregational Transformation.* Valley Forge: Judson Press, 2006.

Lawless, Chuck. *Discipled Warriors: Growing Healthy Churches That Are Equipped for Spiritual Warfare.* Grand Rapids: Kregel Academic, 2002.

Logan, Robert E. *Beyond Church Growth: Action Plans for Developing a Dynamic Church.* Grand Rapids: Fleming H. Revell, 1990.

Longenecker, Harold. *Building Town and Country Churches: A Practical Approach to the Revitalization of Churches.* Chicago: Moody Press, 1973.

Macchia, Stephen A. *Becoming a Healthy Church: 10 Characteristics*. Grand Rapids: Baker Books, 1999.

Macchia, Stephen. "Health Checkup: Ten Telltale Signs of Church Health" *Leadership a Practical Journal for Church Leaders* Volume XVIII (Spring 1997): 36.

MacDonald, Gordon. *Who Stole My Church: What to Do When the Church You Love   Tries to Enter the Twenty-first Century* Nashville: Thomas Nelson, 2007.

Malphurs, Aubrey. *Advanced Strategic Planning: A New Model for Church and Ministry Leaders*. 2nd. ed. Grand Rapids: Baker Books, 2005.

_____. *Pouring New Wine into Old Wineskins: How Change a Church without Destroying It.* Grand Rapids: Baker Publishing Group, 1993.

Mann, Alice. *Can Our Church Live: Redeveloping Congregations in Decline*. Herndon, Virginia: The Alban Institute, 1999.

Martin, Kevin E. *Myth of the 200 Barrier: How to Lead Through Transitional Growth.* Nashville: Abingdon Press, 2005.

Marquart, Kurt E. "Some Aspects of a Healthy Church Life." Lutheran Theological Journal 3, no. 1 (May 1, 1969): 14-135. ATLA Religion Database with ATLASerials, EBSCOhost (accessed February 2, 2010).

McCarty, Doran. *Leading the Small Church.* Nashville: Broadman Press, 1991.

McConnell, Scott. *Multi-site Churches: Guidance for the Movement's Next Generation.* Nashville: B&H Publishing Group, 2009.

McConnell, William T. *Renew Your Congregation: Healing the Sick, Raising the Dead.* St. Louis: Chalice Press, 2007.

McCutcheon, Michael. *Rebuilding God's People: Strategies for Revitalizing Declining Churches.* Camp Hill, PA: Christian Publications, 1993.

McGavran, Donald A., and Peter C. Wagner. *Understanding Church Growth.* Grand Rapids: Wm. B. Eerdmans Publishing Co., 1990.

McGavran, Donald Anderson, and Win Arn. *Ten Steps for Church Growth.* 1st ed. San Francisco: HarperCollins Publishers, 1977.

McIntosh, Gary L. "A Critique of the Critics," *Journal of Evangelism and Missions* Volume Two (Spring 2003): 37-50.

McIntosh, Gary. *One Size Doesn't Fit All: Bringing Out the Best in Any Size Church.* Grand Rapids: Fleming H. Revell, 1999.

_____. *Staff Your Church for Growth: Building Team Ministry in the 21st Century*. Grand Rapids: Baker Books, 2002.

_____. *Taking Your Church to the Next Level: What Got You Here Won't Get You There*. Grand Rapids: Baker Books, 2009.

McIntosh, Gary, and Robert L. Edmonson. *It Only Hurts on Monday: Why Pastors Quit and What You Can Do about It*. Carol Stream, IL: ChurchSmart Resources, 1998.

McMullen, Shawn, and Mary Elizabeth Hopkins. "Common Size, Uncommon Impact," Outreach, July/August, 2006.

McMullen, Shawn. ed. *Releasing the Power of the Smaller Church*. Cincinnati, OH: Standard Publishing. 2007.

_____. *Unleashing the Potential of the Smaller Church: Vision and Strategy for Life- Changing Ministry*. Cincinnati, OH: Standard Publishing. 2006.

McNeal, Reggie. *The Present Future: Six Tough Questions for the Church*. San Francisco: Jossey Bass, 2003.

Miles, David. *ReTurn Resource Kit: Restoring Churches to the Heart of God*. Carol Stream, IL: ChurchSmart Resources, 2005.

Miller, C. John. *Outgrowing the Ingrown Church*. Grand Rapids: Zondervan Publishing House, 1986.

Miller, Kevin A. "Church Health: Developing a Vital Ministry." Leadership 18, no. 3 (June 1, 1997): 21. ATLA Religion Database with ATLASerials, EBSCOhost (accessed February 2, 2010).

Munton, Doug. *Seven Steps to Becoming a Healthy Christian Leader.* Sisters, OR: VMI Publishers, 2004.

Murray, Stuart. 2001. *Church Planting: Laying Foundations* Scottsdale, PN: Herald Press, 2001.

Murrow, David. *Why Men Hate Going to Church.* Nashville: Thomas Nelson Books, 2005.

Myers, Gary. "Stetzer Highlights Keys to Church Revitalization," http://www.baptistcourier.com/2057.article (accessed October 10, 2010).

Neighbor, Jr., Ralph W. "It's the Structure, Period," *Leadership a Practical Journal for   Church Leaders* Volume XVIII (Spring 1997): 36-37.

Nixon, David F. *Leading the Comeback Church: Help Your Church Rebound from Decline.* Kansas City, MO: Beacon Hill Press, 2004.

Nixon, Paul. *I Refuse to Lead a Dying Church.* Cleveland, OH: The Pilgrim Press, 2006.

Oaks, Fred. "Renewing Older Churches," *Leadership a Practical Journal for Church Leaders* Volume XXVI (Fall 2005): 47-49.

Ogden, Greg. *The New Reformation: Returning the Ministry to the People of God.* Grand Rapids: Zondervan Publishing House, 1992.

Ogne, Steve and Tim Roehl. *TransforMissional Coaching: Empowering Leaders in a Changing Ministry World.* B&H Publishing Group, Nashville, TN. 2008.

Oldenburg, Ray. Editor. *Celebrating the Third Place: Inspiring Stories about the "Great Good Places" at the Heart of Our Communities.* Harlowe & Company, New York. 2001.

Olson, David T. *The American Church in Crisis.* Grand Rapids: Zondervan, 2008.

O'Malley, J. Steven. *Interpretive Trends in Christian Revitalization for the Early Twenty First Century.* Emeth Press, 2011.

Ortlund, Anne and Ray Ortlund. *You Don't Have to Quit: How to Persevere When You   Want to Give Up!* Nashville: Thomas Nelson Publishers, 1994.

Ott, E. Stanley. *Twelve Dynamic Shifts for Transforming Your Church.* Grand Rapids: William B. Eerdmans Publishing Company, 2002.

Owen, Marvin. "25 Signs of a Healthy Church" *Deacon*, Spring 2008.

Page, Frank with John Perry. *Who Can Save the Incredible Shrinking Church?* Nashville: B&H Publishing Group, 2008.

Partner, Daniel. Ed. *The Essential Works of Charles Spurgeon: Selected Books, Sermons, and Other Writings.* Uhrichsville, OH: Barbour Publishing, Inc., 2009,

Patton, Jeff. *If It Could Happen Here: Turning the Small-Membership Church Around.* Nashville: Abingdon, 2002.

Pearle, Bob. *The Vanishing Church: Searching for Significance in the 21st Century.* Garland, TX: Hannibal Books, 2009.

Pierson, Robert D. *Needs-based Evangelism: Being a Good Samaritan Church.* Nashville: Abingdon Press, 2006.

Powell, Paul W. *Shepherding the Sheep in Smaller Churches. Dallas*: Annuity Board of the Southern Baptist Convention, 1995.

Preston, Gary. *Pastors in Pain: How to Grow in Times of Conflict.* Grand Rapids: Baker Books, 1999.

Quicke, Michael J. *360 Degree Preaching.* Baker Academic, Grand Rapids, MI. 2003.

Quinn, Robert E. *Deep Change: Discovering the Leader Within.* San Francisco: Jossey Bass, 1996.

Rainer, Thom. *Autopsy of a Deceased Church: 12 Ways to Keep Yours Alive*. Nashville: B&H Publishing Group, 2014.

Rainer, Thom. "Five Major Trends for Churches in America" http://www.churchcentral.com/blog/Five-major-trends-for-churches-in-America (accessed October 6, 2010).

Rainer, Thom S. *Breakout Churches: Discover How to Make the Leap*. Grand Rapids: Zondervan, 2005.

_____. *High Expectations: The Remarkable Secret for Keeping People in Your Church*. Nashville: B&H Publishing Group, 1999.

_____. "Seven Sins of Dying Churches," *Outreach*, November/December, 2005.

_____. "Seven Sins of Dying Churches," *Outreach*, January/February, 2006.

_____. *Surprising Insights from the Unchurched and Proven Ways to Reach Them*. Grand Rapids: Zondervan, 2008.

_____. *The Unchurched Next Door: Understanding Faith Stages as Keys to Sharing Your Faith*. Grand Rapids: Zondervan, 2003.

Rainer, Thom S. and Daniel L. Akin. *Vibrant Church: Becoming a Healthy Church in the 21st Century.* Nashville: Lifeway Press, 2008.

Rainer, Tom and Eric, Geiger. *Simple Church: Returning to God's Process for Making Disciples.* Nashville: Broadman & Holman Publishing, 2006.

Rainer, Thom S. and Sam S. Rainer III. "Coming Home," *Outreach*, July/August, 2007.

_____. "Reaching the "Hard-core" Unchurched," *Outreach*, November/December, 2008.

_____. "The Essential Church Expects More," *Outreach*, July/August, 2006.

Reeder III, Harry L. with David Swavely. *From Embers to a Flame: How to Revitalize Your Church.* Revised and Expanded Ed., Phillipsburg, NJ: P&R Publishing Company, 2008.

Reeves, Thomas C. *The Empty Church: Does Organized Religion Matter Anymore?* New York: Touchstone, 1996.

Regele, Mike, with Mark Schultz. *Death of the Church.* Grand Rapids: Zondervan Publishing House, 1995.

Reid, Alvin L. REVITALIZE Your Church Through Gospel Recovery. Gospel Advance Books, 2013.

Ricketson, Rusty. *Follower First: Rethinking Leading in the Church.* Cumming, GA: Heartworks Publications, 2009.

Riley, Linda. "When Your Wife Resents Your Call," *Leadership a Practical Journal for Church Leaders* Volume XXVI (Fall 2005): 51-55.

Rizzo, Dino. *Servolution: Starting a Church Revolution Through Serving*. Zondervan, Grand Rapids, MI. 2009.

Robertson, Paul E. "Theology for the Healthy Church." *Theological Educator: A Journal of Theology and Ministry* no. 57 (March 1, 1998): 45. ATLA Religion Database with ATLASerials, EBSCOhost (accessed February 2, 2010).

Rosenberg, Joel C. and T. E. Koshy. *The Invested Life*, Carol Stream, IL: Tyndale House Publishers, 2012, 87-88.

Roxburgh, Alan J. and Fred Romanuk. *The Missional Leader: Equipping Your Church to Reach a Changing World*. Jossey-Bass, San Francisco, CA. 2006.

Scazzero, Peter. *Emotionally Healthy Spirituality*. Integrity, Franklin, TN. 2006.

Schaller, Lyle E. *Activating the Passive Church: Diagnosis & Treatment*. Nashville: Abingdon Press, 1982. (Out of print but can be found by Amazon.com)

_____. *44 Questions for Congregational Self-appraisal*. Nashville: Abingdon Press. 1998.

_____.*44 Steps Up Off the Plateau.* Nashville: Abingdon Press, 1993.

_____. *44 Ways to Increase Church Attendance.* Nashville: Abingdon Press, 1988.

_____. *Small Congregation, Big Potential: Ministry in the Small Membership Church.* Nashville: Abingdon Press. 2003.

Schnase, Robert. *Five Practices of Fruitful Congregations.* Nashville: Abingdon Press, 2007.

Schwarz, Christian A. *Natural Church Development: A Guide to Eight Essential Qualities of Healthy Churches.* Carol Stream, IL: ChurchSmart Resources, 1996.

Scott, Marvin. *25 Reasons Why Small Churches Aren't Growing.* Longwood, FL: Xulon Press, 2006.

Sellon, Mary K., Daniel P. Smith and Gail F. Grossman. *Redeveloping the Congregation.* Herndon, VA: Alban Institute, 2002.

Shanks, Carol. *Choosing To Be A "What If" Church: One Church's Story of Revitalization.* CreateSpace Independent Publishing Platform, 2011.

Shelley, Marshall. "Double-Digit Churches," *Leadership a Practical Journal for Church Leaders* Volume IV (Fall 1983): 38-49.

Sjogren, Steve. *101 Ways to Reach Your Community.* Colorado Springs: NavPress, 2001.

Slaughter, Michael. *Spiritual Entrepreneurs: 6 Principles for Risky Renewal.* Nashville: Abingdon Press, 1996.

Smith, Daniel P. and Mary K. Sellon. *Pathway to Renewal: Practical Steps for Congregations*, Herndon, Virginia: The Alban Institute, 2008.

Smith, Ebbie. *Growing Healthy Churches: New Directions for Church Growth in the 21st Century*, Dallas: Church Starting Network, 2003.

Smith, Efrem, and Phil Jackson. *The Hip-hop Church: Connecting with the Movement Shaping Our Culture.* Downers Grove, IL: InterVarsity Press. 2006.

Southerland, Dan. *Transitioning: Leading Your Church through Change.* Grand Rapids: Zondervan, 1999.

Spader, Dan, and Gary Mayes. *Growing a Healthy Church.* Chicago: Moody Press, 1991.

_____. "Growing a Healthy Church," *Leadership a Practical Journal for Church Leaders* Volume XVIII (Spring 1997): 38.

Spurgeon, Rev. C. H. *Sermons of the Rev. C. H. Spurgeon of London*, New York: Sheldon Blakeman and Company, 1857.

Stanley, Andy. *Visioneering*. Sisters, OR: Multnomah Publishers, 1999.

Steinke, Peter L. *Congregational Leadership in Anxious Times: Being Calm and Courageous No Matter What.* Herndon, VA: The Alban Institute, 2006.

Stetzer, Ed and David Putman. *Breaking the Missional Code: Your Church Can Become a Missionary in Your Community.* Nashville: B&H Publishing Group, 2006.

Stetzer, Ed, and Mike Dodson. *Comeback Churches: How 300 Churches Turned Around and Yours Can Too.* Nashville: B. & H. Publishers, 2007.

Stetzer, Ed and Thomas S. Rainer. *Transformational Church: Creating a New Scorecard for Congregations.* Nashville: B&H Publishing Group, 2010.

Stone, Charles. *Ministry Killers and How to Defeat Them: Help for Frustrated Pastors* Minneapolis: Bethany House Publishers, 2010.

Strachan, Owen and Kyle Idleman. *Risky Gospel: Abandon Fear and Build Something Awesome.* Nashville: Thomas Nelson, 2013.

Surratt, Geoff. *Ten Stupid Things That Keep Churches from Growing: How Leaders Can Overcome Costly Mistakes.* Grand Rapids: Zondervan, 2009.

Surratt, Geoff, Greg Ligon and Warren Bird. *The Multi-Site Church Revolution,* Grand Rapids, MI: Zondervan, 2006, 2.

Suirratt, Geoff, Greg Ligon, and Warren Bird. *A Multi-Site Church Road Trip: Exploring the New Normal.* Grand Rapids: Zondervan, 2009.

_____. *The Multi-Site Church Revolution: Being One Church in Many Locations.* Grand Rapids: Zondervan, 2006.

Sullivan, Bill. *New Perspectives on Breaking the 200 Barrier.* Kansas City: Beacon Hill Press, 2005.

Sullivan, Bill M. *Ten Steps to Breaking the 200 Barrier.* Kansas City: Beacon Hill Press, 1988.

Swindoll, Charles R. *The Church Awakening: An Urgent Call for Renewal.* New York: FaithWords, 2010.

Terry, John Mark. *Church Evangelism: Creating a Culture for Growth in Your Congregation.* Nashville: Broadman & Holman Publishers, 1997.

Thumma, Scotty. Travis, Dave. *Beyond Megachurch Myths: What We Can Learn from America's Largest Churches.* San Francisco: Jossey-Bass, 2007.

Towns, Elmer L. "The Beginning of the Church Growth Movement," *Journal of Evangelism and Missions* Volume Two (Spring 2003): 13-19.

Tucker, Sonny. "The Fragmentation of the Post-McGavran Church Growth Movement" *Journal of Evangelism and Missions* Volume Two (Spring 2003): 21-35.

Turner, Emil. "Some Observations on "Church Splits" in the Arkansas Baptist State Convention," *Journal of Evangelism and Missions* Volume Seven (Spring 2008): 27-35.

Vannoy, Karen and John Flowers. *10 Temptations of Church: Why Churches Decline and What To Do About It.* Abingdon Press, 2012.

Viola, Frank and George Barna. *Pagan Christianity: Exploring the Roots of Our Church Practices.* Tyndale House Publishers, 2002.

Wagner, C. Peter. *Strategies for Church Growth: Tools for Effective Mission and Evangelism.* Ventura, CA: Regal Books, 1989.

_____. *The Healthy Church.* Ventura: Regal Books, 1996.

Walrath, Douglas Alan. *Leading Churches through Change.* Nashville: Abingdon Press, 1979.

Warren, Rick. "FIRST PERSON: Forget church growth, aim for church health." *Baptist Press* http://www.bpnews.net/bpnews.asp?id=13131 (accessed October 15, 2010).

Washington, Rev. Dr. John Edward. *The Church Stimulus Package: Jump Start Your Ministry and Revitalize Your Church.* Bloomington, IN: AuthorHouse, 2010.

Wells, Barney, Martin Giese, and Ron Klassen. *Leading Through Change: Shepherding the Town and Country Church in a New Era.* St. Charles, IL: ChurchSmart Resources, 2005.

Werning, Waldo J. *12 Pillars of a Healthy Church.* St. Charles, IL: ChurchSmart, 2001.

"What Does a Healthy Church Look Like?" *Leadership a Practical Journal for Church Leaders* Volume XVIII (Spring 1997): 34-35.

White, James Emery. *Rethinking the Church: A Challenge to Creative Resign in an Age of Transition.* Grand Rapids: Baker Books, 1997.

White, Michael and Tom Corcoran. *Rebuilt: Awakening the Faithful, Reaching the Lost, and Making Church Matter.* Ave Maria Press, 2013.

Whitesel, Bob. *Growth by Accident, Death by Planning: How not to kill a Growing Congregation.* Nashville: Abingdon Press, 2004.

Winseman, Albert L. *Growing an Engaged Church: How to Stop Doing Church and Start Being the Church Again.* New York: Gallup Press, 2009.

Wood, Gene. *Leading Turnaround Churches.* St. Charles, IL: ChurchSmart Resources, 2001.

Wood, Gene and Daniel Harkavy. *Leading Turnaround Teams.* St. Charles, IL: ChurchSmart Resources, 2004.

Wood, George O. "Eight Principles to Revitalizing Your Church"

http://www.enrichmentjournal.ag.org/201001_024_8_ principles.cfm (accessed October 10, 2010).

Youmans, Peter. "My Church's Inferiority Complex," *Leadership a Practical Journal for Church Leaders* Volume XXIV (Fall 2003): 78-81.